CAIN
Son of the Serpent

CAIN
SON · OF · THE · SERPENT

DAVID MAX EICHHORN

ROSSEL BOOKS

CHAPPAQUA, NEW YORK

ACKNOWLEDGMENTS

Before putting this book into its final form, the writer received many valuable suggestions and criticisms from: Mr. Ben Gallob, Rabbi Roland B. Gittelsohn, Miss Eiga Hershman, Rabbi Sidney B. Hoenig, Mr. Lionel Koppman, Mrs. Lillian Lustig McClintock, Rabbi Emanuel Rackman, Rabbi Edward T. Sandrow, Dr. Morton Seidenfeld, Rabbi Marc H. Tanenbaum, and Mr. Arthur Weyne.

Clothbound, ISBN 0-940646-24-2
Paperbound, ISBN 0-940646-19-6

Second Edition
First Paperbound Edition

Book design by Sidney Solomon
Cover design by Shai Zauderer

CONTENTS

CAIN
Son of the Serpent

FOREWORD TO THE SECOND EDITION

At age twenty-five I decided to prepare to become a writer. I would start at the beginning of the Encyclopaedia Brittanica and the Jewish Encyclopaedia and, for twenty years, i.e., until age forty-five, I would read seriatim a book on every major subject in these encyclopaedias. Then, for twenty years after that, i.e., from age forty-five to age sixty-five, I would write.

At age forty-five I felt I was not yet fully ready, so I continued to read for another five years. By age fifty I had completed letters A and B in the encyclopaedias. I determined to write a book on the first article that interested me under the letter C in the Jewish Encyclopaedia. That decision was, for *Cain: Son of the Serpent,* its genesis, its first day of creation. The book's title was the brain-child of my clever and lovable wife, Zelda.

Having spent twenty-five years preparing to write, I reasoned that, the good Lord permitting, I was entitled to spend at least that same amount of time in writing. In the twenty-five years following the completion of *Cain,* I wrote seven more book-length manuscripts, of which, thus far, five have been published. None of these is as uniquely precious to my wife and myself as my first-born volume.

Therefore Zelda and I are delighted and honored that Rossel Books is publishing this second edition of *Cain: Son of the Serpent.*

David Max Eichhorn
Satellite Beach, Florida
3 Nisan 5745 / March 25, 1985

CAIN
Son of the Serpent

CAIN: SON OF THE SERPENT is a midrash.

What is a midrash?

A midrash is an intense exploration of a Biblical verse or a Biblical passage for the purpose of discovering and analyzing the spiritual meaning of that verse or passage. It is not merely a scholarly exercise. It is a method of widening and deepening one's understanding of the theology and philosophy of Judaism. It is, indeed, an exalted form of religious literary criticism and analysis.

Historically, the midrashic process dates back to the fifth pre-Christian century. At about the mid-point in that century, Ezra the Scribe began to interpret for his followers portions of the Pentateuch, also known as the Torah. Torah is a term which has a number of meanings—it may refer to the Pentateuch or to the entire Bible or to the study of Jewish religion and culture or to knowledge in general. Its most frequent and popular Jewish usage, however, is as a synonym for the first five books of the Bible.

As the conviction spread among the Jews that their Torah was divinely inspired, holy, and eternally unchangeable, they began to study it with great zeal and devotion. By the end of the second Christian century, the entire Bible as we now have it was regarded as sacred and as a God-given microcosmic reflection of all that has been, is, or ever will be. Ben Bag Bag, a

Palestinian sage of this period, expressed the prevailing sentiment: "Turn the Torah over and over in your mind, for everything is in it. Think continually about it; grow old and gray in its service and move not away from it; for there is no finer way of life than this." This belief intensified the Jewish determination to discover every hidden meaning in every Book from Genesis to Chronicles. At first, this vigorous investigative process was known as "midrash Torah," "the analysis of the Torah." Later the term was shortened to the single word "midrash."

Practically all the midrashic material which has accumulated through the centuries is found in three places: in the Talmud, in the Midrash, and in the commentaries, medieval and modern, on Bible, Talmud, and Midrash. The word "midrash" (with a small "m") refers to midrashic material found anywhere in Jewish classical religious literature. The Midrash (with a capital "m") is a specific title for a series of collections of midrashic interpretations of each book of the Bible, collections which were compiled and published between the third and thirteenth Christian centuries.

CAIN: SON OF THE SERPENT, then, is a midrash. It is a link in an unbroken chain of Jewish spiritual searching which began somehow and somewhere in the long, long ago, which was given a new form and a fresh impetus by Ezra the Scribe in the fifth pre-Christian century, which has been carried forward for almost twenty-five centuries through the Bible, Talmud, Midrash, and the commentaries thereto, and which will continue to grow and to develop, so far as we now know, indefinitely.

* * *

The classical Midrash, in the form in which it is printed and studied, consists of text, commentaries, and super-commentaries. This format is employed in this book. It has a text and a commentary. Both text and commentary seek to recreate the style and the spirit of the classical Midrash, as nearly as these may be recreated after transference from Hebrew to English language and idiom.

The style of the Midrash is simple and direct. Its spirit is a fascinating combination of mysticism and rationalism, of an all-embracing, completely-accepting religious faith and the down-to-earth, unfettered, audacious, challenging use of reason. An interweaving of fantasy and fact, the interplay of emotions and intellect, a rationalistic philosophy and a complete surrendering of self to God's law and God's will: these are the most striking characteristics of the Midrash and the substance of its beauty and its power.

The writers of the Midrash are not concerned about the truth or the untruth of the fascinating tales which they build on the foundation of the Biblical narrative. The story-telling is merely an attention-getting device, an instrument through which they present to their people the spiritual way of life set forth in the Bible and tested by many centuries of historical experience. The midrashist picks up a Biblical statement, elaborates upon it, and develops from it an ephemeral tale that teaches an eternal truth.

The Jew regards the Talmud as a fence of law which he has built about the Bible in order to guard its sacred doctrines. The Midrash, too, is a kind of protective fence, a fence of interwoven rationalism and mysticism, which seeks to preserve the precious and eternal verities of Judaism. There is always the danger, as is mentioned herein, that the un-comprehending may look upon these fences as being more important and more holy than the truths which they are meant to keep inviolate.

Many learned Jews underestimate the theological and philosophic value of the Midrash. They look upon it as be-ing merely a weird mixture of exotic fairy tales and clever bon mots, useful only, after proper expurgation, for entertaining children in the religious school or providing clever anecdotes for lecture or sermon. They have no deep and clear under-standing that fable, story, and wise saying are only an orna-mental façade, an attractive lure, if you will, to draw the mind's attention to a religious philosophy that demands and de-serves the fullest intellectual consideration and concentration.

The authentic midrashist studies the interpretations given each verse of the Bible by former generations of scholars and he seeks to carry forward the line of thought developed in the Midrash. Study of Midrash does not give one the privilege or the right to produce strange and bizarre explanations of Biblical texts. The genuine midrashist remains within the stream of thought of the Midrash, within the boundaries of the interpretations that have been approved by former gen-erations.

Some look upon the Midrash as a hodge-podge. It is not. The Midrash has a fixed theology and a fixed philosophy. It looks upon God and the Torah and the Jew and the world and their relationships to each other from a solidly estab-lished intellectual and spiritual position. There are many varieties of midrashic treatment of the same theme; there are many types of examples to illustrate the same point; there are shadings of opinion with regard to essentials; there are differences of opinion with regard to not-so-essentials; but these shadings and these differences always remain within the understood theological and philosophic limits. In its own unique way, the Midrash presents to the Jew and to the world a consistent, rational, consecrated pattern of thinking and of living.

* * *

CAIN: SON OF THE SERPENT is a midrashic interpretation of but one chapter of the Bible, the fourth chapter of the book of Genesis, the chapter which tells the life-story of Cain, first-born son of Eve. The various legends and teachings concerning Cain and his family have been woven together to form a connected and coherent narrative. Such literary continuity is not found in the original Hebrew sources, which lie here and there, like the scattered pearls of a broken necklace, amid heaps of other precious midrashic gems. In the appendices at the end of the book, there is a page-by-page listing of the main midrashic source or sources upon which various sections of the narrative and commentary are based and there is also a composite list of all the Talmudic and Midrashic passages and the works of the commentators that were used in binding this story together.

The interspersed sections of interpretive comment in the book contain some of the writer's own thoughts as well as those of outstanding medieval and modern Biblical, Talmudic, and Midrashic exegetes. There has been a determined effort on the part of the writer to keep his opinions within the frame-work of the Midrashic approach to life.

If the pearls of this particular midrashic necklace have

been reassembled and rearranged in such a way that they give a sense of pleasure to those who are charmed by literary aesthetics and a deepened understanding and faith to those who are searching for truth, the purposes of the writer will have been accomplished.

A TYPICAL PAGE OF THE MIDRASH

ON THE OPPOSITE PAGE is a photostatic reproduction of a page from the Midrash Rabba (The Great Midrash), largest and most important of all the classical Midrash compilations. The portion shown is the conclusion of Chapter 21 and the beginning of Chapter 22 of Bereshis (Genesis) Rabba, together with the notes of six medieval commentators. The heavy type at the top is the main Midrash text. The smaller-type printings below are the writings of the various commentators.

Bereshis Rabba is one of the oldest of the Midrash collections. It dates, conservatively, from no later than the sixth century. There are some who date its composition as early as the fourth century.

The commentaries shown were written at various times and in various countries, the oldest in France in the eleventh century and the most recent in Poland in the nineteenth century.

פרשה כא

א ויאמר ה' אלהים הן האדם היה כאחד ממנו וגו'

פרשה כב

א והאדם ידע את חוה אשתו וגו'

מסורת הבדרש

חדושי

רש"י

ידי משה

יפה תואר

דרך

מתנות כהונה

פירוש מהרז"ו

משנת דרבי אליעזר

(מדרש רבה בראשית)

IT WAS SIX A.M. on Friday, the sixth day of the first month, in the year one.

For five days God had been hard at work, creating the Earth and all that is in it, bringing into being an instrument which would add meaning to His existence. Out of Nothing He had summoned light and darkness. To the light He had given the name of Day and the darkness He called Night. Then He had formed the sky, the land, and the sea. He had made the land luxuriant with burgeoning autumnal grass and flowers and trees. He had brightened the sky with sun and moon, stars and planets. He had filled the air with birds and the sea with fish. All of this in just five days.

During the period from sunset to dawn of the sixth day, God created all the animals. All the animals, that is, except Man. The making of Man was delayed until the other animals had been created; for Man was to be their ruler. Man was to represent God on Earth. Man was to be a unique combination. Man was to be part-animal and part-God. No other animal was granted this privilege.

At six a.m. on Friday, the sixth day, God began to make Man. During the first hour, He collected bits of soil from all parts of the Earth. During the second hour, He moistened the soil so that it became, in His hands, as clay in the hands of a potter. During the third hour, He shaped Man's body. During the fourth hour, He filled Man's body with breath. During the fifth hour, He transformed the clay into flesh and blood. At eleven a.m., six hours after the task was begun, the making of Man was finished.

God put the first man, Adam, created full-grown, into the Garden of Eden, a beautiful spot in which grew every variety of vegetation that was good to look upon and to eat. The Man is known as Adam because, in Hebrew, Adam means "red," the color of the clay from which he had been made. God said to Adam, "All the fruit of the Garden may be eaten, with the exception of the fruit of this one Tree. If you ever eat of the fruit of this Tree, you will die."

At God's command, the wild creatures of the Garden were then summoned before Adam to receive appropriate names. After examining the beasts carefully, Adam gave each one the name best suited to his appearance and personality. At the conclusion of the naming ceremony, all the animals marched past Adam in a parade of matching pairs of males and females.

This sight filled Adam with a sudden and frightening loneliness. "Every creature on earth except me has a companion," he cried. "O God, give me a companion, too." God replied, "You are right. It would not be pleasant for Man to live by himself. I shall remedy this lack immediately."

At noon, God caused Adam to fall into a deep sleep. During the next few moments, He performed the first painless surgery in recorded history. He removed one of Adam's ribs and, from the rib, He created a fully developed female. He brought the female to Adam, who looked at her with disgust because she was not pretty and because she was covered with slime and blood. When God saw that Adam was not pleased with his new companion, He took the female away, put Adam back to sleep, and made from and for him another adult female or Woman. It seems that He must have created Woman from a portion of Adam's tongue, for, from that day to this, men's tongues have moved more slowly and more painfully whenever they have been placed in competition with the tongues of women. This Woman, known as Eve, which means "the one in whom life is fashioned," was clean and beautiful in form and in face, pure of heart, innocent in mind. This time Adam was well satisfied with the result of the operation.

Greatly pleased to have someone with whom to share his spacious home, Adam led Eve about the Garden, showing her its plants and its animals and explaining to her the name and nature of each. When the pair came to the Tree whose fruit was forbidden, Adam cautioned Eve, "This Tree you must not touch and its fruit you must not eat. If you violate these instructions, you will die."

Why did Adam tell Eve that she was neither to touch nor to eat? God had only said that the fruit was not to be eaten. He had said nothing about touching the Tree. Adam added to the words of God not out of meanness but out of kindness. He sensed that Eve might be tempted to disobedience more easily than might he. He did not believe that the force of reason exercised as powerful an influence over Eve as it did over him. He felt that he was stronger in mind and in will than was she and, consequently, she would have to be given extra physical and spiritual safeguards in order that she might be protected against any physical or spiritual force which would seek to do her harm. It was because of his affection for Eve and because of his desire to do that which he thought was best for her welfare that Adam tried to improve upon the wisdom and will of God.

It was now one p.m. of the sixth day of creation. The tour of the Garden had been completed. The happy couple sat down in the glade where stood the Tree with the forbidden fruit and, innocently and playfully, began to make love. They smothered each other with kisses and caresses. Gradually, as their dormant passions became more fully aroused, they clung to each other so closely that they became literally one flesh. And they were both completely naked and neither one of them was the least bit ashamed.

The animals who passed by and witnessed their love-making were fascinated by the sight. This was something about which they had had no previous intimation either from God or from Adam. Adam could hardly be blamed for this for he, too, was learning for the first time of the ecstatic joy of physical love. The animals watched intently and reacted speedily. Soon they, too, would be enjoying the delights of that intimacy of male and female which is universal in nature and singular in end-purpose. Soon they, too, would be obeying the Divine impulse to be fruitful and multiply and fill the earth.

Among those who observed this public demonstration of what was to be regarded, henceforth, as an act to be performed in strictest privacy was the Serpent. He was fired instantly with an intense desire to embrace Eve in the same manner in which Adam was engaged in embracing her. He determined, then and there, to move as quickly as circumstance permitted toward the fulfillment of that desire.

Who was the Serpent? The Serpent was the personification of the Evil Inclination. He represents, in this exposition, the self-centered and primitive point of view that the sexual relationship is primarily the gratification of an individual urge and only secondarily the fulfillment of a social responsibility. Those who are controlled by the Good Inclination know that both of these elements enter into any satisfactory act of mating. However, if a choice must be made, in this or any other moral involvement, the welfare of society must always take precedence over the desire of the individual. This is a part of what the Jew means when he says that, in the genuinely righteous man, the Good Inclination has overcome the Evil Inclination. In later days, the Evil Inclination was believed to have its permanent embodiment in a fallen angel or in Satan or in the Angel of Death. In the story of Adam and Eve, the Evil Inclination is personified in the Serpent.

What did the Serpent look like? Some say that he was tall and thin like the giraffe. Others say that he was bent over and humped like a camel. Another opinion is that he looked like the African gorilla or, perhaps, the Malayan orang-outang.

While there is some difference of opinion with regard to the Serpent's physical appearance, there is general agreement on the following points: The Serpent looked like an animal and talked like a man. He was the most clever of all the animals. Had he used his persuasive talents constructively, he would have been second only to Adam in the animal hierarchy. He had a very jealous nature.

Even before Eve was born, the Serpent had witnessed an incident which made him very envious of Adam and his

God-given superior rank. After placing Adam in the Garden shortly after eleven a.m., God, ever the perfect Host, ordered His ministering angels to set before His newly arrived guest a banquet of roasted meat and chilled wine. This, God reasoned, would help Adam to recover quickly from the ordeal of having been created.

Roasted meat? Where did the angels get roasted meat? They had brought down with them from heaven the meat already cooked and the wine already cooled. And the sages add that the meat which was provided by the angels was not only of top quality but was also strictly kosher.

Now, a little more than an hour later, at one p.m., as the Serpent watched the unfolding of another proof that Adam the God-animal was to be supreme among beasts even as he is lowest among angels, the Serpent was filled with a jealous, passionate rage. He would have Adam's Woman as his very own, no matter what the cost.

THE GARDEN was peaceful and quiet. The animals had retired into the depths of the neighboring forest, where each male and female pair proceeded to seek out a lair in order to become better acquainted with the new and fascinating pastime that had just been demonstrated by their master and his mistress. Adam was sleeping contentedly on the ground, with his head in Eve's lap. Eve was stroking gently the hair of her lover, idly meditating upon the power of woman to absorb man's strength, her ability to cause his physical desire to increase, to be satisfied, and to melt away.

The Serpent, who had been impatiently awaiting his chance to be alone with Adam's Woman, peeped through the bushes and, after thoroughly surveying the situation, decided that the longed for opportunity was now at hand. Boldly advancing into view, he motioned to Eve to get up and to join him near the Tree. Filled with that naive curiosity and that aversion to the boredom of silence which were to lead so many of her kind into similar adventures in every generation, Eve quietly eased her body away from that of the sleeping Adam and tiptoed across the glade to the waiting Serpent.

From the very beginning, Eve loved to talk. It seems that the Serpent was aware of this fact and quite prepared to take advantage of it. He encouraged the guileless and carefree female to babble to him about many things, about her creation, her new-found sex life, her desire for a warm fur garment like that worn by the mink, the fox, and the beaver, her walk through the Garden with Adam, and, finally, she talked about the warning which Adam had given her concerning the Tree. "We may eat the fruit of every tree in the Garden with the exception of this one. We are not permitted to touch this Tree or to eat of its fruit. Disobedience of this command will be punished by death."

"Nonsense," said the Serpent. "It will not hurt you either to touch the Tree or to eat of its fruit. The reason that God does not want you to come near the Tree is because it was through this Tree that He became Supreme God. This Tree has co-existed with the gods since time began and it will continue to exist as long as time shall be. Every one who eats of the fruit of the Tree obtains the power to rule over the other gods, to create and destroy worlds, to kill and to make alive. Until God ate of its fruit, He was just a god like all the rest but, after He ate, He became ruler of all the gods and creator of this world.

"He does not want you or anyone else to eat of this fruit because He does not want any rivals in the God-business. Every craftsman hates his competitors and attempts to discourage all potential competitors. And, in every profession or trade, the most recent entrant has a decided advantage over those who are long established in the business. The newcomer has youth and strength and ambition which enable him to forge ahead quickly. Therefore, God does not wish you as a rival, because you are so young and beautiful and brilliant and you would add zest and sparkle to the God-business. I can see you now, sitting on a heavenly throne, bringing to life and putting to death and making and breaking worlds with the best of Them!"

If God were as the materialists of Earth, the words of the Serpent would have had an element of truth in them. For it is normal for Earth's materialists to hate each other and abnormal for them to love each other—for each is in business to outwit and to destroy the other. Together they say that they are in business to serve the public interest but, separately, each tries to outdo the other in winning customers and making profits and building commercial kingdoms. Each has no concern for the other. When one hears that another has failed, he merely shrugs his shoulders and thinks, "There, but for the grace of my brain and my ability, go I." Oh, they are a strange lot, these materialists of Earth. Ruthless and cruel to those whom they do not need and to those who get in their way, they are oftimes soft-spoken and gentle with those who support them, kind to their wives and children and relatives, generous in their philanthropies, gifted in their communal leadership.

There is no real goodness in those who seek only after the things of the Earth. Theirs is the heart of the Serpent. Their chief emotions are jealousy and rivalry and hate. Only among those who seek daily for God and His truth and His righteousness and His beauty can genuine goodness be found. The scientist who seeks truth for its sake and not for his sake; the philosopher who seeks reality for its sake and not for his sake; the devoted one who seeks God for His sake and not for his sake: they know and they show what real goodness is. The poet, the composer, the artist who do not care for the world's wealth or the world's applause but live only that they may seek and discover and depict the beauty of word and of sound and of sense: they know and they show what real goodness is. God is not at all jealous of those of Earth who compete with Him in the doing of goodness and righteousness. He respects them and they revere Him.

"Look," continued the Serpent, "I'm not afraid to touch the Tree." With that, he walked over to the Tree and shook it so hard that its fruit was scattered all over the ground. As he approached the Tree, it said to him, "Stay away from me, you wicked one." But the Serpent was not in a state of mind to be frightened by the words of a mere Tree.

He returned to Eve, put his arms around her, dragged her to the Tree and pushed her against it. "See," he cried, "it does not hurt you to touch it. Neither will you be hurt if you eat of its fruit. God is trying to scare you away from this Tree because He knows that, on the day you eat from it, you will become like Him, a Creator and Destroyer of worlds."

Poor Eve was all confused. Her Man had lied to her. He had told her that if she touched the Tree she would die. She had touched the Tree and she was still alive. If what he had told her about touching the Tree was not so, then why was he also trying to keep her from eating its fruit? The Serpent must be right. Adam, knowing the secret of the Tree, must have made up his mind that he, and he alone, would eat of its fruit and become like God. He did not want Eve to share this privilege. "Adam is a thoroughly dishonest person. The Serpent is the only decent and honest being around." So reasoned Eve. And, so reasoning, she reached up and plucked a piece of fruit from the Tree and ate it. And, so reasoning, she allowed the Serpent to run his paws over her body, to pull her gently to the ground, and to make love to her in the same manner as the still sleeping Adam had made love to her.

III.   SOME ADDITIONAL
OBSERVATIONS

Two important conclusions may be drawn from the portion of the Midrashic story which has been told thus far. One is that the sexual urge is always natural and only sometimes sinful. The other is that, if Adam had told Eve the unembellished truth instead of telling her that which he thought was best for her, she might have been spared much agony and abuse. For century after century, in these as in so many other matters of principle and dogma, many so-called philosophers and theologians have been attempting to sell humanity spiritual merchandise of questionable quality.

There are those who, in the name of religion, have tried to convince the world that the whole story of the Tree and the fruit is a euphemistic description of sexual intercourse and that, when the Bible says that Eve gave Adam a piece of fruit to eat, it really means that she enticed him to sin sexually, even as she also had been enticed by the Serpent. These insistent dogmatists maintain that, before the eating of the fruit, Adam and Eve were as devoid of sex-knowledge and sex-experience as new-born lambs. Had they not eaten the fruit, i.e., not had sexual intercourse, they would have lived forever in the Garden of Eden in everlasting sexless happiness and childless bliss. What a sublime fate! Because they ate the fruit, they brought sin, death, and children into the world. Therefore, sexual intercourse is inherently wicked. Hence every human being is conceived in sin and is tainted with sin from birth. Hence, also, as a direct result of the sexual relationship of Adam and Eve, every human being is condemned to eventual earthly death. However, continue these zealous advocates of pristine purity, if in the course of earthly living one accepts a very special kind of theological indoctrination, he rids himself of the taint of the Original Sin and enters the ranks of the elect who, after earthly death, will be with their Maker in His sexless heavenly abode; while those who refuse to believe that the promptings of the flesh are debasing and wicked will, after earthly death, descend into the depths of hell and there forever burn. Judaism considers this widely accepted explanation of the intertwining of sex, sin, children, and death to be both unsatisfactory and unattractive. Jews greatly prefer the Midrashic explanation that Adam and Eve mated in innocence and purity before either one ate of the fruit of the Tree and that, in so doing, they set a good example for the rest of the animal kingdom, present and future. The sexual instinct, properly controlled, is a great blessing. He who looks upon this instinct as something to be repressed and denied is afflicted with a regrettable narrowness of mind and of heart. In eating the fruit of the Tree, Adam and Eve disobeyed a Divine command and, for this misconduct, they were punished. But how can anyone who has known the glow of human love in its most intense physical expression bring himself to believe that this experience is a degrading crime, an everlasting sin, a prelude to death? . . .

It is always much better for one person to tell another the truth just as it is rather than to try to color the truth by telling it as he thinks it should be. God made truth just as it is. And ever since the world began, Man has been unwilling to accept the truth just as it is but he has been trying to improve upon God's way of doing things by adding details which he feels God must have overlooked. Or he may be moved by the modest conviction that he knows more about what is best for his fellow-men than does God. As, for instance, Adam. God said, "Don't eat." But Adam said to Eve, "Don't touch and don't eat." Why? Because Adam felt that he knew more about women than God did. How? Simple. Adam had a wife. God did not have a wife. The inevitable result of Adam's finite logic was that Eve got into worse trouble than if he had told her the exact truth. She became convinced that she could trust neither Adam's judgment nor his veracity. This is what happens when Man tries to protect God.

God's truth, as revealed in nature and in human experience, forms a beautiful garden of the spirit. Man's truth, as expressed in Man's laws and customs, seeks to enclose and protect God's truth, as a fence protects a garden. But sometimes Man builds the fence so high that light can not penetrate the garden and God's truths wither and die. And sometimes Man builds his fence of such unwieldy material that the fence falls in upon the garden and crushes it. Unfortunately, many men who call themselves religious are much more interested in preserving the fence than they are in tilling the garden. They spend so much time mending and painting and reconstructing the fence that they pay no attention to the noxious weeds which are gaining mastery over the garden. Sometimes these so-called religious people are so befuddled by the restrictions they have placed upon themselves that they come to believe not only that God made the fence but even that the fence is more important than the garden. When that happens, beware. Eventually, there must come the realization that practically all of the externals of religions are Man-made and not God-made. In its rebellion against those who have laid too much stress on externals, humanity may reject not only the externals but the central and essential principles of religion as well. This is what happened inside the mind of Eve in the matter of the touching and the eating.

At the end of each of the first five days of creation, God had looked
at His work and had decided that it was good. But, at the
end of the sixth day, when He considered His accomplish-
ments on this day, He declared that they were very good. This
was because, on the sixth day, through the Serpent, evil was
mixed into the good. Good by itself was merely good. But
good mixed with evil was very good.

Were there only good in the world, mankind would not know
that good exists. It is only through the presence of evil that a
human being is able to recognize good when he finds it. Goodness that exists in the midst of evil is the best goodness there is.

When the Serpent wrapped his arms around beautiful Eve and
poured his seed into her eager body, he affected life in two
important ways: Henceforth, willing females would allow
themselves to be captured by even more willing males for
purposes of pleasure and profit as well as for the purpose of
procreation. And henceforth, only pagans, barbarians, and
ignoramuses would speak to mankind about Good and Evil as
if they were absolute and opposite.

All is good, for God is all, and God is good. Evil is good misun-
derstood, good misapplied, good gone wrong. Evil exists only
in the mind of Man. There is no evil in the mind of God. This
is probably the most important law of the universe and one
which, as yet, mankind has utterly failed to comprehend.
Judaism teaches it but many Jews do not yet believe it.

The difficulty is, of course, that too many people, when they evalu-
ate the events of their lives, seem to take it for granted that

(24)

the universe was created especially for them. Such a self-centered theory holds a great appeal for the egotist but, judging from the monotonous regularity with which nature makes and destroys every kind of living organism, it is rationally unsound. Much more realistic and much more sensible is the Jewish point of view that one must attempt to accommodate himself to the world as he finds it rather than expect the world to accommodate itself fully to his human wishes and his human dreams.

Throughout the ages, men have asked, Why do the wicked prosper? Why do the righteous suffer? Why has this happened to me? What have I done to deserve this? Why does one sort of endeavor, which seems to be completely devoid of merit, bring wealth and happiness, blessing and praise, and another, which seems to be worthy in every respect, result in misery and ruin? The answer is very plain: We behold the world through the finite eyes of men and not from the infinite perspective of God. What to us appears to be evil may be, in His sight, very good. We can see no farther than what looks like the next bend in a mysterious and endless road. It is the part of wisdom and of faith to believe that, from God's vantage point, the road is quite straight, thoroughly engineered, and of Divinely determined length. It is also the part of wisdom and of faith to believe that God deliberately created what Man calls Evil in order that human life might really be worth the living.

Eve had eaten of the fruit of the Tree and she had not died. But neither had she become like God. She was neither less nor more of a person than she had been before she ate the fruit. Now she was completely confused. Adam had lied to her, but the Serpent had lied to her, too. She was not dead—as Adam had foretold. Neither was she able to fashion worlds and to demolish them—as the Serpent had predicted.

"Adam is no good and the Serpent is no good," she said to herself. "No male is any good. They just want you for the pleasure you can give them. After they use you, they just push you aside and fall asleep like Adam or walk away like the Serpent. . . . But a female is more clever than any male, though she must never let him know this. She must let him think that she is his slave while, in the same moment, he is obeying her every whim. . . . The Serpent was completely wrong but how may I be sure that Adam was also completely wrong? I have not yet died from eating the fruit, but death may come upon me in an hour from now or a day or a year. And, if I were to die, Adam would get himself another Woman. He would forget that I had ever existed. If I am to die, why should he be allowed to go on living? If I have done wrong, so has he. He lied to me. He should have told me the truth. Adam, my sweet, I shall awaken you and I shall persuade you to eat of the fruit also. We shall live together or we shall die together. How shall I persuade you? Ah, my darling, while you slept, my encounter with the Serpent taught me that we women possess a very charming, interesting, and precious talent. She who uses that talent artfully and judiciously has at her command a weapon of persuasion more powerful than the thoughts of the most wise or the tongues of the most elo-quent. Have I learned my lesson well? That we shall soon discover. . . ."

Adam woke up and, artfully encouraged by Eve, he ate of the fruit of the Tree. Then, still enchanted by the spell of Eve's very special kind of talent, he repeated with her in private the act which, a short time before, they had blithely demonstrated to the animals.

The Evil Inclination was transmitted by the Serpent through Eve to Adam and, through Adam, to the human race. Until the Torah was given to Moses on Mount Sinai, there was no sure way in which the human race could protect itself against the Evil Inclination. This brutish urge, compounded from both physical and social essences, at first filled both men and women with such an intense desire to vent their lusts upon each other that the early generations were deficient in compassion and social conscience and were motivated mainly by selfishness and jealousy. The sea of physical desire surged to the very gates of heaven. It finally enticed certain of the less conscientious angels to give up their angelic privileges and to come down to earth, where mistresses were sought and found among the daughters of men. While this last-mentioned development did not occur until almost the very end of the events to be narrated in this book, it is mentioned here as an indication of the far-reaching results of the introduction of the Evil Inclination into human relationships. Only after receiving the Torah was the people of Israel able to gain a measure of control over the Evil Inclination. It was from the Torah that the people of Israel learned that no one can live only for himself and that each must live for all.

From her initial sexual relations with Adam, Eve did not become pregnant. After receiving the Serpent's seed, Eve became pregnant. From her second act of intercourse with Adam, Eve became even more pregnant.

Some unimaginative twentieth-century biologists will label this last statement unscientific and impossible. In the early days of the world, the storytellers paid little attention to what were to be known later as the laws of nature. Why should one be disturbed because the sages say that Eve nourished in her womb, at one and the same time, two fetuses generated by two entirely different males? Is this any more remarkable than their claim that the world was created from Nothing or that the earth's vegetation was in full bloom when it came into being or that Adam and Eve were ushered into existence not as mere infants but as fully grown adults? Modern science boasts continually of the great marvels it has wrought through its complicated formulae and mechanical devices. It has not yet come anywhere near the miracles which the ancients were able to perform simply by stretching their imaginations. . . .

How great is the power of the Evil Inclination! From the very beginning, sexual curiosity was aroused innocently but lust produced pregnancy and children. Were human beings to wait until they were moved by social considerations before they started to create families, eventual racial suicide would be a very likely prospect. It is not eagerness to serve society, to maintain an ancient tradition, or to do one's bounden duty that leads most youths and maidens to the marriage altar and the domestic hearth. It is much more likely to be a warm body, a skin which is smooth and soft to the touch, rippling muscles, a friendly smile, a tender kiss. The emotional and the intellectual and the spiritual feed upon and build upon the physical. In the titillating game which the sexes play with each other in order to satisfy their respective physical love-hungers, the Self must first be appeased before the Socius begins to function acceptably.

The refusal of society to recognize and accept this is one of the great tragedies of our time. Until intelligent social steps are taken, the already too-high divorce rate will continue its disagreeable climb. Young couples contemplating marriage must be granted the right to assure themselves, sensibly and decently, that their union will be based on a bed-rock of physical attraction and satisfaction which no amount of petty quarreling or economic misfortune or family interference will be able to shake. It would be much more spiritual for the pure of heart to admit that some of their century-old moral prejudices are no longer functioning effectively in our present-day society than for these straining pietists to continue to condemn unnumbered millions of men and women to life-long marital unhappiness and servitude.

Sometime after two p.m. on Friday, the sixth day of the first month, in the year one, Eve gave birth to Cain and a twin-sister. Before three p.m., she gave birth to two more children, Abel and a twin-sister. All the children were also born as full-grown adults. Because of the shortage of human beings on the earth at this time, Adam allowed each of the sons to mate with his own twin. In later generations, such incestuous unions were forbidden under penalty of death but, in these early days, necessity outweighed all other considerations. Adam was very understanding. When the girls were born, he could have claimed them for himself, since they had been developed on (or, more accurately, in) his property. However, wisely foreseeing the unpleasant personal and social consequences of a family situation in which one man possessed three young women and two other males, able and willing, had none, and recognizing that rugged individualism is less desirable than social harmony, Adam graciously permitted his sons to retain possession of their bosom companions.

There is nothing in the record to indicate that Eve ever told Adam anything about her affair with the Serpent. Nor does she seem to have been aware that the Serpent, and not Adam, was the father of Cain. It is quite clear from the record that both Adam and Cain believed firmly that their relationship to each other was that of natural father to natural son.

THE BIRTHS of the two sets of twins filled Eve's heart with joy. "Now," she thought, "now my husband will never leave me. He will stay with me to the end of my life. Our children will be a link of love which will bind the two of us together forever."

Foolish woman. Foolish woman dreaming the vain dream of so many of her sisters through the generations. If your husband truly loves you, he will stay with you until death does you part, children or no children. If your husband does not truly love love you, one, two, or ten children will not deter him from deserting you if the provocation is sufficiently strong. And if a sense of duty and responsibility impels him to stay "for the sake of the children," your life will be an endless mental and physical nightmare. For the sake of the children, it might be better oftimes if he is gone than if he stays and stays and stays. It is not pleasant nor healthy to long for the death of another. . . .

There are those among the sages who declare that Adam and Eve set a pattern for all the families of mankind. No home should have less than two children. The literalists insist that there must not be less than two male children. The more indulgent are content to fix the minimum at one male and one female. Some say that the ideal family is one which, like that in Eden, consists of father, mother, two brothers, and two sisters.

Eve's joy did not last very long. Less than two hours after the second twins were born, her hopes for an idyllic future turned to ashes. The voice of God was heard rolling like thunder through the Garden: "Adam, Adam, where are you?" Adam and Eve were filled with a sudden fright. Pushing their children before them, they scrambled into the bushes and hid. "What's the matter with you?" asked the Voice. "Why are you frightened? Have you eaten from the fruit of the Tree?"

Timidly the First Family came out of their hiding-places. "Yes, we did," said Adam. "That Woman You gave me, she worked some kind of magic on me and I ate." "Is that so?" the Voice asked the Woman. "Yes," said Eve. "The Serpent persuaded me to eat and then I persuaded my husband to eat."

Then the Voice said to the Serpent: "You have exceeded your authority. I gave you permission to tempt but not to fall victim to your own temptations. Woe unto the spellbinder who swallows his own words! He shall be doubly cursed and doubly punished. Most loathed of creatures shall you be, O Serpent. Upon your belly shall you crawl and dust shall be your food. Women will pull their garments more tightly together in your presence. They will shrink from your touch. Men will hunt you down and crush you without pity and without remorse."

And to the Woman the Voice said: "Because of your lack of trust in your husband, because you allowed your emotions to run riot over your intellect, because your standards of judgment were false and your powers of investigation weak, from now on you shall bring forth children painfully and in pain shall you rear them. Your husband shall be your master mentally and physically and only with guile shall you be able to overcome him."

And to Adam the Voice said: "Because you disobeyed My command, because your physical appetite was stronger than your spiritual endurance, because, in the first crisis of your brief existence, the animal within conquered the God within, you shall be like the animals in every way but two. Like the animals, you shall be born, breed, and die. Like the animals, you shall grub in the dirt for your food and you shall work to build your lodging. Like the animals, you will eventually merge with the dust from which you were taken. Your place and your time will see you no more and future places and future times will not know that you ever existed. But, like God, you will have a mind and, through your mind, you may become, for a brief moment in history, a king or a lunatic and, sometimes, both. And, like God, you will have a sense of humor and the ability to laugh, the ability to laugh at yourself and at your kind and at a world which, in the end, will swallow you up and reduce you to physical nothingness."

And to all of them the Voice said: "Get out of this Garden and never come back."

It was now five p.m. of the sixth day of the first week of the first year of Earth's history. Twilight was beginning to fall. In another hour, the first Sabbath, the first Day of Rest, would begin. To leave the Garden so late in the day would involve desecration of the Sabbath. Out of the circle of the Heavenly Family came the Angel of the Sabbath. "O God," she prayed, "during the first six days of Creation, You have been doing everything You could to guarantee Man health and ease of mind and body. And now, on the seventh day, the Sabbath Day, the very day which You have set aside for Man as an especial day of rest and contentment, You are going to violate the Sabbath spirit by forcing Man to leave the Garden! Is this the special holiness of my Day? Is this its special honor? Is this what Your Torah means when it says, Genesis 2:3, that 'God blessed the seventh day and sanctified it'? Is this an example of Your wisdom and Your justice?"

Moved by the plea of the Sabbath Angel, God granted the First Family permission to remain in the Garden until Saturday night, the conclusion of the Sabbath. And would God be so unjust as to drive out these homeless refugees on Saturday after dark, when they could not see where they were going and could not find a comfortable place to lie down and when the wild beasts of the forest might sneak up on them and tear them to pieces? Of course not. God's final word was that He would allow them to delay their going until Sunday morning.

As the sun went down gradually behind the horizon and darkness began to creep over the world, Adam's heart was filled with fear. Like a terror-stricken child, he cried out to his Heavenly Father: "Woe is me! Because of my sin, the world is becoming dark and it will soon return to the oblivion from which it came. This is the death that God has decreed for me and my kind because of my wickedness." All that night, Adam did not move from his place. He did not sleep. He sat and shook with fright and with grief. His wife sat at his side. She, too, was afraid of the dark and she, too, sobbed and cried. When the dawn came, they jumped up and embraced each other joyously for now they knew that darkness is not to be regarded as a punishment nor as a sign of the end of the world. Rather it is a daily testing of hope and of faith and a sign of the end of one day's world and the beginning of another on the morrow.

Early Sunday morning, the fugitives gathered together their few possessions, and the whole family, Adam and his wife, Cain and his wife, and Abel and his wife, left the Garden and journeyed toward the east.

The sages say that it was God's original intention to live on earth with Man. When Adam sinned, the spirit of God left the earth and went up to the first heaven. When Cain sinned, He went to the second heaven; when the generation of Enosh sinned, to the third heaven; when the generation of the Flood sinned, to the fourth heaven; when the generation of Babel sinned, to the fifth heaven; when the Sodomites sinned, to the sixth heaven; and when the Egyptians sinned in the days of Abraham, to the seventh heaven. Abraham brought the spirit of God back to the sixth heaven; Isaac to the fifth; Jacob to the fourth; Levi to the third; Kehas to the second; and Amram to the first. Moses and the Torah brought God back from heaven to earth.

THE FIRST FAMILY moved eastward, out of the Garden, into
the wilderness and the desert.

From the earliest days, wilderness and desert figure prominently
in the history of the Jew. That which is worthwhile in Judaism
has been developed through a long process of simple, lonely,
painful living. Only in times of adversity, destitution, and
affliction has Judaism produced its greatest prophets, poets,
philosophers, dreamers. Material ease has been, for the Jew,
spiritual dis-ease. When he finds wealth and social acceptance,
his mind turns away from the teachings of his fathers and his
heart ceases to be attuned to the heart of God. When he is
miserable and troubled, his words sparkle, his thoughts deepen,
his spirit is aglow with the flame of inner dedication. The Jew
clings more closely to God in the darkness, the wilderness,
and the desert. The eternal verities which he offers humanity
he has begotten in agony and self-denial. Everlasting happiness is not for him.

Cain became a farmer. Abel became a shepherd.

There was deep significance in their choice of occupations.
Cain was an indecent materialist. He was determined to get for
himself as many worldly possessions and as much worldly

power as he possibly could. He was not concerned about the spiritual welfare and future of either himself or the human race. What would happen to him or to his kind after he was dead was, for him, a matter of no importance whatsoever. The here-and-now and what's-in-it-for-me were all that counted. Therefore, he selected farming as his occupation because real estate is the most tangible of all earthly assets. A piece of land is the kind of property which is most difficult to steal and most difficult to destroy.

The Midrash rates the farmer very low in the occupational scale. Farmers are considered to be selfish, quarrelsome, narrow-visioned. The three characters in the Bible who took up farming seriously all came to a bad end: Cain a murderer, Noah a drunkard, and King Uzziah a leper. All three were punished because they abandoned the way of God and put their trust in earthly goods. They idolized material property and material values and physical strength and power. But shepherds and cattle-raisers are different.

Shepherds are regarded as idealists. They live out in the wide open spaces, out in God's country. They are not confined to any one bit of land. They wander about as free men. They live a peaceful, idyllic life. They do not concern themselves overly much with the acquisition of material possessions. Theirs is a serene, contemplative existence, close to nature. Cattle-raising is considered by many of the sages as the finest of occupations and cattle-raisers as the finest of people. It is remembered that Israel's greatest Biblical leaders, Moses and David, spent their formative years in the wilderness herding oxen, goats, and sheep. This is the way, then, that a good man prepares himself for the Godly life: by separating himself from material temptations, by living simply, by developing within himself the power of inner contemplation and the joy of inner contentment. The sages believe that Abel displayed wisdom and strength of character when he decided to become a shepherd rather than a farmer.

However, from the very beginning of history, it has been apparent that, in our world, absolute victory rests neither with the shepherd nor the farmer, neither with the idealist nor the materialist. Neither can ever hope to gain complete mastery over the other and neither can live completely without that which the other cherishes.

Cain busied himself with growing plants and crops on the ground which he owned. Abel was also kept very busy taking his herds out to pasture, milking his cows, and shearing his sheep and goats. The farmer and the shepherd enriched each other's lives by exchanging their surplus products. Cain bartered his excess vegetables and grains for Abel's wool, milk, butter, and cheese. The slaughtering of animals for human use and consumption was not permitted until the time of Noah, so that Abel was only allowed to use the skins and meat of animals which died a natural death. This law prevented Abel from stocking up on hides and meat. Therefore, he supplied these particular items to Cain in rather limited amounts.

Though the brothers made use of each other's skills and merchandise, this was not sufficient to keep the temper and tempo of their relationship on an affectionate level. Cain was a quarrelsome, jealous chatter-box. He seized every possible occasion to try to create difficulty for his brother. Cain looked and acted exactly as one would expect a son of the Serpent to look and to act. Abel, on the other hand, was by nature a peaceful and quiet man. He had been created, on his father's side, in the image and likeness of God and this noble lineage was evidenced in the innate goodness of his character. Not that Abel was perfect. No son of Eve was or ever could be perfect.

On one occasion, Cain aroused his brother's ire by his uncompromising insistence that farming is the most important of all human occupations or preoccupations. The farmer grows the food through which mankind nourishes itself. He grows the linen and the cotton from which mankind spins its cloth and makes its garments. Therefore everyone has need of the farmer. But the farmer has no real need for anyone else. He could, if necessary, get along all by himself, without the help of any other living creature.

Abel replied, with some heat, that raising cattle and sheep and goats was much more interesting and much more rewarding than sowing handfuls of seed and planting bulbs and threshing grain and picking corn. A bulb does not rub itself affectionately against your hand when you water it and a field does not look at you with eyes of love when you scratch its back. The herdsman deals with living things whom he loves and who love him. The relationship between the farmer and his crops is a very impersonal, a very crass one. How many bushels of wheat will I get from this field? How much money will I lose if I don't get rid of these plant lice? But the love of a shepherd's dog for its master, the pride of a herdsman's horse in its rider, the well-mannered devotion of a flock of sheep, the gentleness of a herd of cows, the sprightliness of a young goat: what does the dirt-farmer have to match these daily joys?

The sages say that God Himself has settled this argument in the most convincing of ways. In the Bible, God refers to Himself a number of times as a Shepherd but never once does He call Himself a Farmer!

THE MONTHS of the first year of the world's existence began to roll by. As the first autumn and the first winter became history, Cain and Abel labored diligently at their chosen tasks. Their efforts were blessed by God with much success. Cain's fields began to yield an abundant harvest from the seed which he had sown. Abel's cows, ewes, and goats gave birth to fat, healthy calves, lambs, and kids in large numbers.

On the eve of the fourteenth day of the seventh month, at the beginning of the first spring season, Adam approached his sons. "Tonight we must show our gratitude to God," he said, "by offering Him a sacrifice of our choicest possessions upon an altar which we shall build. In future ages, our descendants will sacrifice a lamb each year on this very night at this very spot as a thank-offering for a great deliverance from slavery which God will give to them. We shall show by our act of thanksgiving that, had it been our lot to live in that time of future redemption, we, too, would have been worthy of being liberated."

Adam's sons proceeded to build an altar, as their father had instructed them. God was greatly pleased, so pleased, in fact, that it was upon that very same altar, many generations later, that Noah offered up an ox, a sheep, a goat, and a pair of doves to celebrate his deliverance from the Flood and that

Abraham bound Isaac, when the first Jew was commanded by the Almighty to sacrifice his only son whom he loved so dearly.

Adam was the first to come to the altar. He brought with him a unicorn, which he placed upon the altar and killed by cutting its throat with a knife. Thus was instituted the now universal custom of taking the lives of animals and human beings, when the taking of such life brings some sort of benefit, imagined or real, temporary or permanent, legal or illegal, to some other animal or human being, to a social organism, or to a god or God. After the animal was dead, Adam lighted a fire under it and watched until it was wholly consumed, for, as has been stated, the eating of the meat of a slaughtered animal was forbidden until the time of Noah.

Why a unicorn?

Some of the sages say that Eve's earlier intuitive suspicions with regard to Adam were well grounded, that, at the very beginning of his life, Adam was, indeed, a pagan. He did not believe that God had created the world nor that He controls the world. He believed that the world is eternal and that God had become the most powerful Force in it by eating of the fruit of the Tree. He thought that God did not want Eve and himself to eat from this Tree lest they become as powerful as He. After Eve and he had eaten from the fruit of the Tree and been punished for so doing, Adam recognized that his theory with regard to the potency of the fruit was wrong. And after his first experience with the darkness and the dawn, Adam became certain that God was older and more powerful than the world, that He had created it and He controls it.

Therefore, in the first sacrifice which Adam offered to God, he tried to symbolize his new religious faith. Just as a unicorn has but one horn, so, too, Adam now believed that there is and can be but one God. Just as this horn points straight upward, so, too, Adam now believed that He Who dwells in Heaven above controls the world. And just as this one horn is placed in the middle of the forehead, directly in front of the brain, so, too, Adam now believed that the God Who controls the world is not a capricious or cruel deity but is One Who governs His domain with wisdom, with justice, and with love. This is what some of the sages say about Adam and the unicorn.

Cain was the next to bring his offering. He walked up to the altar and nonchalantly tossed upon the top of it a fistful of wild flax-seed.

Abel did not arrive with his sacrifice until almost the very end of twilight. He was so anxious to give to God the very best of his possessions that he had gone through all his pasture-grounds, herd by herd, to make sure that he had selected from each the prize first-born. Just as his father and brother were beginning to believe that Abel had decided not to bring a sacrifice, Abel came into view, leading a procession of fine little animals, a heifer, a young sheep, and a young goat.

Bringing his animals up to the altar, Abel noted with amazement the worthless offering of his brother. "My brother," Abel cried out, "is this the way you show your gratitude to God? By throwing in His face a handful of seeds that grow wild in your fields? Do you think this is the proper manner to give Him thanks for the abundance He has given you?"

"You are being hyper-critical and hypocritical," his brother answered. "You had no intention of bringing anything at all until you found out what father and I were going to offer. You were jealous of us. You were afraid that God would cease to care for you. So you went out and got all these animals together to make sure that you would not be outdone by us."

Abel looked at his brother for a moment in silence. Then he said, "God will judge both the givers and their gifts, my brother."

He bound up the feet of his precious animals, lifted each gently to the top of the altar, and then turned away. He walked back to where his father and brother were standing. No sooner had he reached them than the whole area was lighted up as with a light of brightest noon-day. A bolt of fire descended from the skies and, in an instant, the animals which Abel had placed upon the altar disappeared completely. But the wild flax-seeds were not touched! They were not even singed.

Thus did God make known His opinion with regard to the givers and their gifts. In the brilliant light of the heavenly fire, the face of Abel brightened like that of an angel. But Cain's face became ugly. It burned with the dark redness of one who seethes with anger. It changed from red to white and back to red again, as does the face of one who has been greatly humiliated and deeply hurt.

Who can blame Cain for feeling as he did? From the point of view of an indecent materialist, what crime had he committed, what wrong had he done? What right did God have to shame him in so public a manner? There is no greater or deeper feeling of hurt than that which takes root in an outraged scoundrel.

What does a thorough-going materialist think that he owes to God or to society? If one lives for himself alone, what, in his opinion, does he owe anybody? But if you grant him his premise and ask him, in return, what anybody owes him, he scowls and snarls like a caged beast, for that is what he is, one who is imprisoned by his own conceits and by the narrowness of his social vision.

Cain was a typical representative of that portion of the human race which believes that the world has been created to satisfy its particular needs and desires. The logical consequences of such a philosophic position are unbounded selfishness and inevitable social conflict. Such people are easily identifiable. They fancy themselves all-important and all-wise. They are always the first to sit down at the table and the last to offer to wash the dishes. They give to charity not out of compassion and to religion not out of thankfulness but to gain recognition or to avoid ostracism. They have no use for anyone who cannot be of some use to them. In their Book it says: "Thou shalt love thyself first, last, and all the time, and to hell with thy neighbor!"

That kind of thinking sometimes produces an abundant material harvest but it also breaks hearts and spirits and creates human misery. And sometimes it is the heart and spirit of the materialist that gets broken. If one digs deeply enough under the thick hide, he finds a heart in the toughest of them and, somewhere within that hardened exterior, there is what some refer to as a conscience and others as a soul. They have their tender spots, be it their pocket-book or their golf-score, or, perhaps, a favored sweetheart or an only child. They can be hurt, they can be checked, they can be broken, but seldom can they be changed. Let the moment of alarm or restraint pass away, let their fortunes again take an upward turn, and the old conceit and the old arrogance are again on display.

It is difficult, perhaps impossible, for the Cains to understand why they are rejected by both God and history. Technically they do no wrong. They stay, rather precariously sometimes, within legal bounds. They observe just enough social amenities and fulfill just enough social responsibilities to get by. They do what they have to do with no social feeling and no sense of spiritual communion.

Sometimes they try to buy their way to family affection and social acceptance. Sometimes this stratagem meets with superficial success. Their wives, children, mistresses, nieces, nephews, cousins, servants, secretaries, business associates, social companions, parasites, and other roommates, shopmates, and clubmates respect their power, fear their wrath, envy their wealth, and cater to their every whim with outer grace and inner loathing. And sometimes they bluff, bull, bellow, brag, or buy their way to positions of communal leadership. One meets them in all manner of guises, perhaps as a legislator or as president of the local Chamber of Commerce or as the director of a bank, yes, perhaps, even as the most prominent member of the governing board of a church or synagogue. They often win temporary worldly victories. They never achieve a permanent spiritual triumph.

Love and respect cannot be bullied nor bought from either man or God. They must be earned. As long as the world endures, it will be the idealists and not the materialists, the Abels and not the Cains, who will earn for themselves that love and respect which is both human and divine. Abel brought God the best that he had, in humility and in joy, with no mental reservations whatsoever, eager only to serve, to worship, to be accepted, to be loved. His was the open mind and the open heart, a mind which knew no guile and a heart which beat in unison with the Heart of the universe. He not only gave back to God part of that which God had given to him, but he also dedicated to God something which he himself had created, something which it was not in God's power to give, a spiritual treasure of reverence and devotion which belonged to him alone.

Back of every gift stands the spirit and the character of a giver. No matter how beautiful a proffered gift may be, God does not accept it unless the soul of the giver is equally beautiful. God was favorably impressed with both Abel and his offering but neither Cain nor his offering was pleasing in the sight of the Lord.

Cain: Son of the Serpent

The Biblical prohibition against having woolen and linen threads woven into the same garment, Deuteronomy 22:11, is explained by the sages as follows: No Jew is ever to wear a garment in which are interwoven threads of wool, made from the sheep, one of the animals of Abel's acceptable offering, and threads of linen, which are made from flax-seed, the unacceptable offering of Cain. This will serve as a constant reminder that the idealist must never allow the indecent materialist to corrupt him and to turn him away from his devotion to God's law.

VIII.   "SIN CROUCHES AT
THE DOOR"

ABEL WAS greatly disturbed by the dramatic manner in which
God had indicated His pleasure with his offering and His dis-
pleasure with that of his brother. Abel felt very sorry for Cain.
He had no desire to see him humiliated. After all, Cain was
the elder brother and, even in those early days, it was understood clearly that the oldest boy in the family carries a larger
share of family honors and family responsibilities than the
younger children. Abel tried in every way that he could to
convince Cain that this was just a temporary set-back and
that he would soon be restored to God's favor.

But Cain was angry, deeply and dreadfully angry. He was
so angry that he was in no mood to listen to words of love,
of comfort, or of wisdom. Cain felt very sorry for himself.
Everything and everybody was against him. God had been
very unjust. God had given no advance indication whatsoever
of the importance He would attach to the offering. And Abel's
deliberate plot to supplant him as God's favorite was unforgivable. Now Abel would receive all the blessings which God
bestows on men and he would receive nothing. Now he and
his descendants would be relegated to the role of second-
class citizens in the world while Abel and his descendants
would be the rulers of mankind. Abel had gotten in his way,

maliciously and cruelly. Such wickedness must not go un-challenged. He would find a way somehow to set matters aright and to restore himself to the position of prominence and authority which had been his before Abel's diabolical connivings had upset the scheme of things.

God was aware of the storm that was raging in Cain's mind and He knew only too well what evil consequences might ensue if such dark brooding was not checked. "You are being very unreasonable," said God to Cain. "If you will stop acting like a child and start behaving like a sensible person, you will have a more important role than Abel in world history, for, after all, you are the elder brother. Abel loves you. He has no desire to dominate your life and he will gladly follow your leadership.

"What has happened has happened and what is done is done. No good can come from anger, disappointment, or dejection long contained. Through a harsh and bitter experience you have been taught that Man's relationship to Me is a very important part of life, a relationship which he must have in mind constantly and never treat profanely nor lightly. If, in the future, you try to please Me, that which is past will not be held against you. But, if your present mood of resentment and hate continues, beware! Sin is crouching at the door of your heart!"

The verse of the Bible in which this last speech of God is im-bedded is one of the most peculiarly worded verses in all of Scripture and, at the same time, one of the most profound. The Talmud says that this verse, Genesis 4:7, is one of five verses in the Bible whose grammatical construction is so un-usual that they are very difficult to translate.

According to the interpretation of Genesis 4:7 accepted by the majority of our sages, this verse is to be translated as follows: "If you do that which is right, everything will go well with you. But if you continue along your present way, beware! The Evil Inclination is crouching at the door of your heart! However, even the Evil Inclination is hopeful that your better nature will emerge triumphant from this spiritual testing. You can accomplish this if you will try hard enough."

In the story of the Garden of Eden, the Evil Inclination was present in the guise of the Serpent. Here it appears again but in a different form. As has been stated, the Evil Inclination is often embodied, in Jewish tradition, as a fallen angel or Satan or the Angel of Death. It is generally believed that, at this point in the life-history of Cain, the Evil Inclination appeared in the guise of Satan.

Now who is Satan? This is a very important question because the average Jew is not well acquainted with the origin and purpose of the Jewish Satan. The average Jew has been so thoroughly conditioned by non-Jewish thinking on this subject that, if he were asked to identify Satan, he would answer unhesitatingly that Satan is the Devil. And who is the Devil? The Devil, he will reply, is the enemy of God. And what is the Devil's purpose? The Devil's purpose is to cause Man to do evil in contradistinction to God's purpose, which is to cause Man to do good. Is the Devil trying, then, to upset the plan of God? Oh yes. Is the Devil, then, an Evil Power while God is a Good Power? Yes. Is the Devil, therefore, co-existent and co-equal with God? M-m-m-m, no, not exactly. In what way is the Devil not co-existent and co-equal with God? Well, until the time of the world's creation, he was one of the leading angels in Heaven, but, after the world was created, he led a rebellion in Heaven against God and, because of this, God cast him out of Heaven and he became God's perpetual opponent, an Evil Spirit, Satan, the Devil. However, in some way which Man cannot yet completely foresee, Satan will wage a last-ditch struggle with God at the end of days and God will triumph over him.

These would be the responses of an average Jew whose thought-processes have been affected by frequent exposure to the traditional Christian teachings on this matter. Those present-day Jews who have not been subjected to such Christian influences would simply state that Satan is the Devil and let it go at that. They would neither know nor care about the career of the Devil because, moved by the logic of intense monotheism, they would have an immediate cognition that belief in such a Devil is unacceptable theologically and scientifically. However, one may be sure that these same Jews, once they have learned about the Jewish Satan of the Talmud and Midrash, will regard him, as did their fathers, with an understanding and not completely unfriendly manner. For the ancient Jewish Satan is not at all like the medieval Christian Devil or the Islamic Shaitan.

The medieval non-Jewish conception of the Devil places those who hold this belief on the horns of a logical and theological dilemma from which there seems to be no escape. If the Devil is so powerful that God cannot cope with him, it is then quite evident that God shares His control of the world with another and there is, in that case, not one God but two, a Power of Good and a Power of Evil. If, on the other hand, the Devil was created by God and yet is so wicked that he is able to thwart God's plans, why does not God get him out of the way by destroying him? If God had the power to create the Devil, He certainly has the power to destroy him. If God is All-good, why does He permit the Evil One to continue to exist and sometimes to triumph?

This dilemma hounds the medieval believer in the Devil because his kind of religion is essentially and overwhelmingly egocentric. His primary concern is to save the soul of the individual so that that individual may spend eternity in Paradise. Therefore, when he grapples with the problem of Good and

Evil, he centers his attention upon personal sin, personal salvation, upon what is good or bad for the individual. Judaism, on the other hand, has always, in ancient, medieval, and modern times, placed the main emphasis on the welfare of society and not on the welfare of the individual. Judaism has always maintained that what may now appear to be evil to or for the individual is quite likely to result ultimately in social good. Judaism has always maintained likewise that, in the long run, what is good for society is good for the individual and that the ultimate test of an individual's worth is the extent to which he is willing to suffer personal discomfort and humiliation in order that his fellow-men may have the good life more abundantly.

In the final analysis, nothing is entirely without good for God is All-good and, therefore, God would not permit anything which is pure evil to exist. This basic Jewish concept has already been affirmed in this book. It bears repeating at this point because of the relationship between the Jewish concept of Satan and the Jewish attitude toward sin.

It is well to record that, in our time, a substantial number of non-Jews have divested themselves completely of the medieval obsession with regard to individual salvation. These unfettered minds are busying themselves more and more with the task of helping to build a more nearly perfect social order right here on earth, a task to which Judaism has been dedicated from its formative years.

The Jewish Satan is an enemy neither of God nor of Man. He was created by God deliberately to serve as the official tempter of mankind. There is no virtue in being merely good. To be truly virtuous, one must have been given a choice between the good and the evil and must have chosen the good. Satan is God's instrumentality through which Man is given the opportunity to sin or to conquer the urge to sin. When Satan is assigned the task of tempting a certain individual to sin, he does not, of course, announce his presence nor does he appear in a manner or a costume that is unpleasant or readily recognizable. He conceals his identity through the use of all kinds of disguises, most of which are intentionally very attractive. He may appear on earth, for example, as a mink coat, a uranium stock, a ten-thousand-dollar bribe, an unlimited expense account, or even as the beautiful wife of one's best friend.

According to Jewish tradition, Satan is a very useful member of God's administrative staff. His task is definitely on the unpleasant side and his efforts are not always appreciated by those whom he seeks to help. In this he is not alone. There are times when this same description applies, in equal measure, to many other more highly respected persons: parents, school teachers, judges, and law-makers, to name just a few.

Satan does not rejoice when his efforts to induce a man to sin meet with success. Quite the contrary. His heart swells with joy only when his utmost efforts are of no avail and his most enticing offers are disdainfully rejected. He hopes that his earthly opponents will overcome and conquer him because he knows that this will cause them to find favor in God's sight.

When words of Torah are being discussed, Satan comes as close as he can to the discussants without being obtrusive so that he may listen, for he greatly enjoys learned discussions. At times he even tries to take part in the discussion, usually by attempting to relate the topic being discussed to some juicy piece of current gossip or to a revised version of an ancient bawdy joke. This technique occasionally has a very disquieting effect on the course of the deliberations. What is to be done then? The opinion of the sages is divided. Rabbi Chanina bar Papa says: "Stop the levity immediately. Get back to serious business. Drive the intruder out." Rabbi Simon takes a kindlier and perhaps a more realistic attitude. He says: "If Satan comes to have fun with you when you are engaged in a scholarly task, entertain him with words of Torah. If you do so, God will give you as much credit as though you had helped Him create two worlds, the world of heaven and the world of earth, for you will have shown that you have an understanding of that which is human as well as of that which is divine."

On one day every year, Satan loses his power to tempt men to sin. This is on Yom Kippur, the Day of Atonement. The numerical value of the Hebrew term for Satan is 364. Satan can cause trouble for humanity for 364 days each year. But on the 365th day, Yom Kippur, Satan takes a holiday.

IX. THE EVIL INCLINATION: SERVANT OR MASTER?

Is Man conceived in sin and is he by nature evil? There are religions which say "Yes." Judaism says "No."

There is no wickedness in an unborn child. If an unborn child suffers, it is because of the weaknesses of society or of its father or mother. Unborn children suffer because of the iniquities of a society which does not provide enough bread and milk, which makes the innocent pay the price for the mistakes of the indifferent, which equates the law of Man with the will of God. Unborn children suffer because one or both parents failed to keep their bodies clean, their minds clear, their desires disciplined. There is no wickedness in an unborn child.

Man is innately good. He cannot be otherwise because he was created by God Who is All-good. Evil exists only because God realizes that, without it, Man's life would lack meaning and purpose. If Evil were not, Man's earthly experience would be a continual, monotonous piling up of goodness upon goodness. Evil constitutes a challenge to Man. It makes his life interesting and purposeful. Therefore, God deliberately created Evil. If God so desired, He could destroy Evil this very minute. But there is not much likelihood that He will so desire for a long, long time. Evil still has a very important role to play in the gradual unfolding of the life-cycle of the human race.

God has placed in the soul of Man both a Good Inclination and an Evil Inclination. This is another way of saying that God has given to Man the privilege of choosing between the good and the evil.

(53)

What is the Evil Inclination like? It has already appeared in our
narrative in the likeness of the Serpent and of Satan. What is
it like? What is its nature? How does it act? What is its usual
manner of approach? How may it be recognized? The sages,
in attempting to answer these questions, employ many similes
and comparisons.

The Evil Inclination, they say, does not enter a man's life as a
huge, overpowering force. Its beginnings are small, humble,
unspectacular. Rav says that it is like a little insect which
lodges in the vital organs of a big animal and ultimately causes
the animal's death. Samuel says that it is like a little seed
blown by the wind which gets caught in the crevice of a rock.
The seed develops slowly into a full-grown tree which splits
the rock in two. It is like a flea, whose bite is weak and which
cannot enter into healthy flesh. But, wherever it finds a small
hole in the skin, it has sufficient strength to enter and to lay
its eggs. When the eggs hatch and the fledgling fleas emerge,
they enlarge the hole so that it becomes eventually a festering
sore. So it is with the Evil Inclination. As soon as one deviates
just a little from the path of righteousness, he has opened the
door of his heart to the Evil Inclination. A door which is
tightly closed is difficult to open, but a door which is slightly
ajar is easy to open the rest of the way.

Rabbi Berachia says that at first the Evil Inclination is as weak
as a woman and later becomes as strong as a gladiator. At
first one is tempted to commit only minor misdeeds but he
has started down a road which may end in shame and death.
Rabbi Akiba says that each sin is initially like the threads
of a spider's web but that, as one's heart becomes hardened to
wrong-doing, he gradually enmeshes his spirit in a twisted
cord of evil as thick and as strong as the rope which anchors
a ship or pulls a wagon.

Rabbi Isaac says that, when the Evil Inclination first appears, he
disguises himself as an invited guest but that, if he is permitted
to remain long enough, he becomes the master of the house. It
is like the parable told by the prophet Nathan to King David

after the king had made love to Bath Sheba, the wife of Uriah the Hittite, Second Samuel 12:4, "And there came a wayfarer unto the rich man, and the rich man did not take food from his own flocks and herds for the traveller, but he took the poor man's sheep and prepared it for the man who had come to him." The Evil Inclination comes first as a "wayfarer," one who just happened to wander by, then as a "traveller," one who makes frequent journeys into the neighborhood, and finally it reveals itself as "the man who had come to him," as one who is going to remain permanently. The Evil Inclination approaches as one humble in spirit, seeking lodging, with malice toward none and with gratitude toward all who show him kindness. Gradually his attitudes and demeanor change, until, at last, after he is in complete control of the situation, his true nature is revealed in all its ruthlessness and cruelty. As one becomes more accustomed to the habit of doing wrong, he becomes more bold, more callous, more lustful, less careful, less humane, less likely to obtain forgiveness.

The Evil Inclination is very clever. Rabbi Tanchum bar Marion says that it accomplishes its objectives with the same kind of devious strategy that marks the maneuvres of the dogs of Rome. In Rome a dog sits down in the market-place near a baker's stall on which are heaped many loaves of bread. The dog pretends to fall asleep because he knows that the baker does not trust him and that, until the baker is quite certain that he (the dog) is asleep, he (the baker) will not take a nap. When the baker's head begins to droop and he begins to snore, the dog jumps up and scatters the heaped-up loaves of bread all over the street. While the startled and still half-asleep baker is slowly concentrating his energies on putting the loaves back where they belong, the dog quickly grabs one of the loaves still lying on the ground and escapes with his loot to a place of quiet and safety where he peacefully eats and fills himself and blesses God for the stupidity of the bakers of Rome.

Rabbi Ammi says that, contrary to the opinions of most people, the Evil Inclination would rather walk down the middle of the main boulevard of a city than lurk in the side streets of its more humble sections. The poor but honest citizens who dwell on the side streets, who believe in the principle of "Live and let live," who get along very well with their next-door neighbors, who share unselfishly each other's moments of happiness and tragedy, are unwilling subjects for the hypnotic attraction of the Evil Inclination. But the ambitious and worldly men who seek the limelight, who lead the parades down Main Street, handshaking the faceless mass and kissing its babies, always reaching out for more and more fame and riches and power, they are the ones at whose side the Evil Inclination marches. Woe unto them and woe unto those who put their trust in them!

Rabbi Abbin concludes that anyone who pampers the Evil Inclination in his youth will have the Evil Inclination for a ruler in his old age.

How may one overcome the Evil Inclination? By the study and the teaching of Torah. In the final analysis, the essence of the Evil Inclination is that it encourages Man to seek his own personal advantage and his own personal pleasure rather than to be moved by a desire to do that which will benefit both his fellow-men and himself. Since the Torah is designed to accomplish exactly the opposite, namely, to encourage Man to work for the well-being of society rather than for his own selfish purposes, it follows that the Torah is the ideal antidote for the poison generated by the Evil Inclination.

Since the Torah was not given to Israel until the time of Moses, it is quite evident that, in the time of Cain, mankind did not possess this valuable antidote. Therefore, God dealt more leniently with pre-Sinaitic sinners than with those who came later. If Cain had been in possession of the teachings of the Torah when he sinned, his punishment would have been much more severe.

However, God did indicate to Cain very clearly that it is in Man's power to overcome the Evil Inclination, to choose the good and to eschew the evil: "If you do that which is right, everything will go well with you. But if you continue along your present way, beware! The Evil Inclination is crouching at the door of your heart! However, even the Evil Inclination is hopeful that your better nature will emerge triumphant from this spiritual testing. You can accomplish this if you will try hard enough."

The desire to do evil is continuously present in the human mind. It is there primarily for the purpose of stimulating and testing Man and not for the purpose of hurting him. The question is not: Is the Evil Inclination crouching at the door of my heart? Of course, it is. The Evil Inclination is at the threshold of my heart and your heart and that of every other living being. The question is: Is the Evil Inclination stationed at the door of my heart as servant or as master? Do I know and control my weaknesses or do my weaknesses know and control me? Through answering these questions carefully and honestly, one determines whether he is a good person or an evil person.

Prior to the giving of the Torah, mankind did not make any concerted effort to counteract the efforts of the Evil Inclination. The early generations were of the opinion that it is useless to attempt to fight against the enticements of the Evil Inclination because they believed that it is God's will that Man shall have no control over the actions of his mind and body. Noah was among the first to understand that this is not so. He chose the good and abandoned that which was evil and obtained mastery, in his own personal life, over the Evil Inclination. However, he did not attempt to teach this doctrine to others. He was interested only in assuring his own present and future salvation. But Abraham was different. Abraham was given an advance insight into some of the principal teachings of the Torah and he tried as diligently as he could to spread these teachings to all parts of the then-known world.

Abraham proclaimed to all who would listen that human nature is not depraved, that the Evil Inclination cannot conquer the genuinely good man, and that God, through giving Man the right to choose between good and evil, has granted Man a share in the determination of his own destiny. For many generations, the Evil Inclination acted as a kind of bully over mankind. And then along came Abraham. As Rabbi Abba says: The Evil Inclination, in that early time, may be compared to a sickly bandit who used to hold up everyone who passed along a certain highway. On one occasion, he held up a man who was not only strong and courageous but also keenly alert. Noticing that the robber was extremely nervous and feeble, the intended victim ended the career of the highwayman by giving him a thorough thrashing. And so it was with Abraham and the Evil Inclination. Abraham arrived on the scene after the Evil Inclination had been bullying humanity for a long while. Although he could not and did not bring the activities of the Evil Inclination to a permanent halt, he did cause the situation to change for the better by administering a thorough thrashing to the false religious theories that were being advanced by his contemporaries.

The Talmud contains the following interesting description of the relationship of the Evil Inclination and the Torah: During the nine months that a child is being developed in the womb of its mother, the fetus spends its time studying the Torah. This protects it against all evil until the time comes for it to be born. As the child emerges from the womb, an angel appears and slaps the child on the mouth so hard that the child begins to cry. At that moment, all the Torah which the child has studied disappears from its memory. For the next thirteen years, the child is at the mercy of the Evil Inclination. Its parents encourage it to relearn all the Torah that it can so that it may ward off, as far as possible, the bad influence of its continual tormentor. If, during these first thirteen years, a youngster profanes the Sabbath or steals or indulges in strange behaviour or commits any other of the thousand and one crimes which are a part of a normal childhood, the child is immediately forgiven, for it is understood that he does not yet possess completely the restraining and protecting guidance of the Torah. But, after the lad becomes a Bar Mitsva, a Son of the Commandments, at the age of thirteen, he is presumed to be sufficiently well-versed in the Torah to withstand the blandishments of the Evil Inclination and to be dominated by the Good Inclination. From this time on, he is held accountable if he celebrates the Sabbath improperly or steals or commits any other of the thousand and one crimes which are not considered a part of a well-disciplined adulthood.

Every day the Evil Inclination presents some kind of temptation to the grown man and grown woman. Such temptations are overcome by the continued study of Torah, by genuine repentance for past wrongs, by daily remembrance of the inevitability of retribution and death, and by the giving of charity. One must also keep in mind constantly that the attempts of the Evil Inclination to induce mankind to sin are part of the Divine plan. It is God's way of finding out whether or not a man is prepared to yield to His will and to obey His law.

Ecclesiastes 7:20, "There is no one living who is so righteous that he does good continually and never sins." When one succumbs to the blandishments of the Evil Inclination, as, at some time or other, every one inevitably must and will, he should not thereafter lose heart completely, give way to despair, contemplate suicide, or indulge in any other of the foolish utterances, thoughts, and acts which indicate a lack of faith in a loving and forgiving God.

When a man sins, he atones for his sin by righteous living. Only that man whose sinning is premeditated, constant, and without remorse will be beyond forgiveness and subject to unavoidable punishment, even though at times the punishment may be long in coming. When proper atonement is made, one's face is lifted up. The sense of shame and of guilt disappears and, in its stead, there arises a heightened sense of the worthwhileness of struggle and the richness of life's challenge.

The Psalmist sings, Psalm 9:2, "I will give thanks unto the Lord with my whole heart." The sages ask: What does it mean to give thanks to God with one's whole heart? It means to thank

God for both the good and the evil, for the lessons He teaches mankind by means of the Good Inclination and by means of the Evil Inclination.

Solomon said, Ecclesiastes 4:13, "Better is a poor and wise child than an old and foolish king." "A poor and wise child": This is the Good Inclination. Why is it called a child? Because it exerts very little influence on a person during the first thirteen years of his life. Why is it called poor? Because not everybody pays heed to it. Why is it called wise? Because it teaches mankind the right way to live. . . . "An old and foolish king": This is the Evil Inclination. Why is it called a king? Because everybody pays attention to it. Why is it called old? Because it is part of everybody's life from the day he is born until the day he dies. And why is called foolish? Because it teaches mankind the wrong way to live.

Rabbi Judah bar Illai once preached a sermon in which he said, "There will come a day when God will bring the Evil Inclination before the righteous and the wicked. In their presence, He will put an end to the existence of the Evil Inclination. To the righteous the creature will look as big as a mountain and to the wicked he will seem like a thread of hair. As the righteous and the wicked observe the destruction of their ancient tempter, both will begin to weep. The righteous will weep and will say, 'How were we ever able to overcome such a monster?' And the wicked will weep and will say, 'Why were we not able to conquer such a puny thing?'"

FOR A TIME Abel kept away from Cain in order to give his
brother an opportunity to put aside his anger and to return to
a more sensible frame of mind. After God spoke to Cain and
pointed out to him the dangerous nature of his continuing
anger, Abel felt sure that Cain would cast off his feelings of
hurt and would resume his normal tasks with the comforting
understanding that, so long as he acted properly, he would
occupy a very high position among God's representatives on
earth. Assuming that this would be so, Abel again began to
associate with Cain as freely as he had before the incident of
the offering had disrupted their brotherly relations.

Unfortunately for Abel, his analysis of Cain's reaction to
God's warning was inaccurate. God's words to Cain served
only to deepen the determination which was already there,
the determination to get rid of his rival brother once and for
all, this brother who was standing between him and the position in life which he was resolved to achieve. Cain's mind
was too much filled with schemes for getting his earthly com-
petitor out of the way to find room for the childish reasoning
of a spiritual Meddler. Why was everybody trying to prevent
him from reaching his destined greatness? Why did he have
to be annoyed by the foolish objections of those who could
not possibly understand that nothing must be allowed to

stand in the way of his march toward the imperial heights of material wealth and world domination?

Cain decided to murder Abel for a number of reasons. The sages state that he did not believe that his parents intended to have any more children. Therefore, with Abel dead, all the future generations of the world would be descended from him. Once his brother was out of the way, Cain and his family would possess and control all of the earth's treasures. If Abel remained alive and first in God's favor, Cain and his descendants would have to be content to play a secondary role in world affairs. Then there was another factor, one which has been among the principal causes of murder from that day to this: a woman. There are those who say that Cain was jealous because Abel's wife was prettier than his own. From the very moment of birth, Cain had wanted Abel's twin-sister. He had insisted that, as the elder brother, he should get first choice of women. But Adam had decided that it would be better for each brother to marry his own twin. This decision was very displeasing to Cain but there was nothing more that he could do about it for the time being. There were others who claim that the first female God had created was still alive and that each of the brothers was intent upon adding her to his family household. However, the majority opinion is that God destroyed this first female before He created Eve and that the only lady who was involved in Cain's determination to commit murder was Abel's wife.

In order to allay any possible suspicion of his ultimate intention, Cain began to shower more outward affection upon his brother than he had ever done before. Instead of addressing Abel by that name, as had been his custom, Cain began to speak of him and to him as "My dear brother." He tried in every way to make Abel think that all was well between them.

But try as hard as he could, Cain was unable to keep completely hidden the tendencies toward quarrelsomeness and argumentation which were so much a part of his natural self. On one occasion, he got into quite a wrangle with Abel over the theological question of reward and punishment. Cain, still smarting under what he considered an unjust Divine decision, contended that God is a capricious Deity Who decides matters of right and wrong according to His mood of the moment. Since He owns the whole world, what difference should it make to Him whether one offers Him flax-seed or the richest gift, since He created and is the Master of everything? Abel insisted that God judges an offering by the spirit of the giver as well as by the amount of sacrifice that is involved in the giving. Cain replied, "My dear brother, your mind is benumbed by a theological opiate which, were it not for sturdy realists like myself, would keep mankind in eternal subjection to an absurd theory. There is a higher Power than ourselves Who created this world but He has no genuine interest in that which He has made. He is neither a righteous Judge nor a wise Law-giver. He will neither reward the good nor punish the wrong-doer. The only kind of justice or of law which we shall ever know is that which we create for ourselves." "When will you understand," responded Abel, "that it was this kind of thinking that got you into trouble before and will do so again if you continue to harbor such an unhealthy point of view?"

Finally Abel began to realize that Cain's perverseness was so deeply imbedded that it was not going to be easy to get his brother's thoughts turned into more constructive channels. Therefore he decided that a more wholesome relationship might be established between Cain and himself if the two of them divided up their properties in such a fashion that each would stay out of the way of the other. At first, Cain insisted that, since he was the elder brother, he should get a double share of everything but, after some argument, he consented to an equal division because of his inner conviction that, regardless of what arrangement was made, everything in the world would soon be his anyway.

The two brothers agreed to draw a line through the middle of the world. Everything on one side of the line would belong to Cain, everything on the other to Abel. Abel realized that this solution was decidedly unfair to Adam but he was willing to enter into any agreement which gave some promise of appeasing Cain. He secretly determined to share his own portion with his father and mother. However, an unanticipated complication arose which caused this plan to be abandoned.

The altar of offering built by Cain and Abel stood on a spot which was at the exact center of the world. A line drawn through the middle of the world would pass directly over the altar. In the days of the Temple, the Even Ha-shesia, the stone on which is engraved the actual name of God, would be set on this very site. It would be located in the very center of the Holy of Holies. The Holy of Holies would be in the exact center of the Holy Temple. The Holy Temple would be at the exact center of Mount Moriah. Mount Moriah would be in the exact center of Jerusalem. And Jerusalem would be located exactly in the center of the world.

Having been given a Divine intimation of the importance of the altar-location, each brother demanded that it be included in his domain. Cain maintained that, as the elder, he was entitled to first choice of any disputed territory. Abel argued that, since God had shown him special favor at this particular place, he should be permitted to possess it. Neither brother would give in and it became necessary, therefore, to seek some other way of promoting fraternal tranquillity.

This time it was Cain who proposed a way of dividing up the world which would be reasonable and satisfactory for both parties. "My dear brother," he purred, "since Nature seems to have endowed us with quite contradictory outlooks on life, I suggest that we divide the world in a manner which accords with our personal philosophies. I am a thorough-going materialist. I believe that the solid substance which makes up Mother Earth is the only genuine reality and, in the final analysis, the only source of genuine wealth. On the other hand, you seem to place more emphasis on the world of the spirit, on values which are not so closely bound to time and place and circumstance. Accordingly, let us divide all property in this manner: I shall take everything that is immovable, everything that is bound to the earth: the land, the grass, the bushes, and the trees. You will take as your portion everything that is movable, everything that is separated from the earth, for these are the less substantial things, the less permanent, the continuously changing. In this way, each of us will possess that part of the world which suits him best and there will be a very clear line of demarcation between that which belongs to you and that which belongs to me."

Abel agreed readily. He was too trusting or too naive to see through the diabolical cleverness of Cain's proposal. Material and spiritual, immovable and movable, indeed! If that which is free to move where it will is never to have any place

to move from or to or on, it does not have very much freedom, does it?

The next day Abel was out in the fields taking care of his
cattle when Cain suddenly appeared before him. "Get off my
property this instant," Cain roared, "and take everything with
you that is yours." Abel looked at him in astonishment. He
began to comprehend that he had paid too high a price for
appeasement. Silently, he turned away from Cain and drove
his cattle to a more remote pasture. No sooner had he gotten
himself well settled than Cain again was upon him. "I told
you to get off my property," he snarled. "Get off immediately
or I will kill you."

Abel's face flushed with sudden anger. "Where do you
expect me to go? It is quite clear that, under our new arrangement, it will be necessary for me to house my possessions on
your property just as it will be necessary for you to make use
of the things which belong to me. It is very plain that it will
be absolutely impossible for either of us to get along without
the other."

"Don't preach me another one of your sermons," Cain
shouted. "Just get off my property. Jump off. Fly off. Leave
in any way that you can but go right now."

"Very well. If you want to get tough, I can get tough, too.
Take off your clothes. They belong to me just as much as this
land belongs to you."

Cain advanced toward Abel menacingly. Abel, still want-
ing to avoid a fight with his brother, turned and ran. Cain ran
after him. Abel kept on running until he came to the summit
of the mountain on which was erected the altar of God. When
he reached this sacred spot, which was, as has been stated, at

the very center of the world, he stopped and faced his adversary.

Like an enraged animal, Cain seized his brother and hurled him to the ground.

They wrestled. Abel was much the stronger and more agile of the two and, in a few minutes, he had Cain pinned beneath him and begging for mercy. "Oh, my dear brother, do not kill me," Cain whined. "Just think of the sorrow and shame you will bring upon our dear father and mother. There are just the two of us in the world to carry on the family name. Why is it not possible for us to get along with each other? How will you ever face our dear parents if you kill me? Oh, my dear brother, let us be friends. Let bygones be bygones. Allow me to get up so that we may embrace each other, as brothers should, with love and with trust."

Abel began to weep tears of relief and of joy. Here, at last, was the new Cain, the brother with whom he could live in peace and brotherly love and harmony. "Of course, my beloved Cain. I have no desire to harm you. Get up and let us once more be friends." And so saying, he released Cain from his grasp.

As Cain arose slowly from the ground, he seized a large rock that was lying near and, clutching it with both hands, he brought it down with all his strength upon his deceived brother's head. He smashed in Abel's skull. Then, filled with blind fury and hate, he hurled himself upon the prostrate form. He choked it with his hands, he kicked it with his feet, he bit it with his teeth as an animal bites its prey. And, finally, taking a sharp stick, he began methodically to pierce Abel's body in many places, from the feet to the head, for he did

(67)

not know in what part of the body the life-giving force is lodged. Only by making certain that the life-giving force went forth from wherever it was could he be sure that Abel was definitely dead. As a coup de grace, he used the stick to cut Abel's throat and sever his wind-pipe, as he had seen his father Adam do when he had offered up the unicorn as a sacrifice. And then he jumped to his feet and ran away. . . .

Abel's blood was splattered all over the nearby trees and stones. But there was no blood upon the ground. Desiring to shield its master Cain, the ground opened its mouth and swallowed every drop of blood of Abel within its reach.

Abel's faithful dog, who had accompanied his master and his master's flocks during the good days that were now forever past, came to stand watch over the body of his lord and friend, even as during the long nights he had guarded the sheep of the slain man.

Adam and Eve came, too. They sat and wept and mourned for their dead son. They did not know just what to do. This was the first time in history that a human being had died. There was no relative, no neighbor, no human person to whom they could turn for guidance in their time of sorrow.

As they sat there, a raven appeared, dragging with it the body of another raven which, like Abel, had just died. As Adam and Eve watched, the raven dug a hole in the ground with its claws and its beak, placed the body of its dead companion in the hole, and then filled up the hole with dirt. In this way, Adam and Eve learned what they, too, must do. Following the example of the raven, they prepared a grave and buried their beloved son.

For having taught mankind how to dispose of its dead, the raven was rewarded by God. What were the rewards which the raven received?

The sages say that once in a while a mother-raven gives birth to a white chick. Since ravens are normally black, the mother of the white chick thinks that she has begotten a baby with an evil spirit and she becomes frightened and abandons the new-born one. Whenever this happens, God takes over the rearing of the forsaken albino and watches over it and feeds it until it is able to care for itself. In addition, whenever the ravens, through their peculiar cry, inform God that the crops need rain, God heeds their call and causes the needed rain to fall.

Upon returning home after the burial, Adam and Eve ate lentils as a sign of mourning.

Why lentils? The sages say that just as lentils are round and, in turning a lentil, one must inevitably come back to the point from which he started, so, too, as one goes through life, he must inevitably experience sorrow as well as joy, And just as the lentil has no opening and no mouth, so, too, a person stricken with grief searches in vain for some outward form of expression through which to give vent adequately to his inner pain. Yes, just as the lentil is entirely closed up within itself, so, too, a really religious person is quiet and composed in moments of anguish because one who has faith in God's wisdom and justice accepts that which is sweet with gratitude and that which is bitter without complaint.

Because through his sin humanity had been condemned to be mortal, Adam felt that he was directly responsible for the murder of his second-born. This had gone far enough.

He had already caused too much suffering and grief. He would cause no more. He would beget no more human children. To have children in a world such as this is a crime. If a child knew what it was going to have to endure, it would resist coming forth from the womb. Parents want children only in order to satisfy their own selfish desires. They never consider the happiness or the unhappiness of the yet unconceived child. If they did, Man would scatter his seed upon the ground rather than risk the possibility of being a partner in the creation of misery and misfortune. No more human children. Adam determined that his love-life with Eve must end. When the period of mourning was over, he gathered together his belongings and left the house. From that time on, Adam lived apart from his wife.

AFTER KILLING Abel, Cain ran away as fast as he could for he did not want to be near when Adam and Eve learned that their younger son was dead. He had not gotten very far from the sacred mountain when God appeared before him.

"From your father and mother you can flee but from Me you cannot flee. Where is your brother Abel?"

"O Master of the universe, why do You ask me such a question? Am I my brother's keeper? I most certainly am not. I have undertaken the responsibility of managing Your fields and Your vineyards but I have not consented to be my brother's overseer. That, O Master, is Your responsibility. You are the Guardian of all creatures and the Keeper of everything that lives. Why do You ask me where my brother is? If You do not know where he is, then You have been derelict in Your divine duty. You are like a house-watchman who discovers that the house which he guards has been burgled. The watchman ferrets out and seizes the thief and says to him: 'Why did you rob my house?' 'Why did I rob your house?' replies the thief. 'Because it is my business to rob houses. But what about you? Where have you been and what have you been doing? It is your business to prevent houses from being robbed. Why were you not pursuing your task as diligently as I have been pursuing mine?' "

Cain was clever but God is also clever. God did not ask Cain where his brother was in order that Cain should give Him the answer. He asked Cain the whereabouts of his brother in order to indicate to Cain that He already knew what had happened to Abel. God, in this instance, may be compared to a policeman who, while walking along a deserted street, comes upon two men. One is lying on the pavement dead. The other is standing over the dead man. "Who killed him?" the officer asks. "You ask me who killed him?" responds the other. "If you, who are the authority on all matters pertaining to law and order, do not know, how can you expect me, one without any official responsibility whatsoever in this matter, to know who did it?" "Now, see here," the policeman answers, "I was not asking you a question so much as I was indicating to you what is in my mind. When I asked you, 'Who killed him?,' I was saying in effect 'You killed him, didn't you?' because you are standing right over him and there is no other person in sight. Your seemingly ingenious response only serves to deepen my suspicion that you are guilty of this man's murder."

Cain, in this situation, may be compared to one who enters another's garden, picks some of his mulberries, and eats them. The owner of the garden comes running after him and demands angrily: "Have you been eating my mulberries?" "I have not." "You are a liar, for your hands are stained with fresh mulberry juice." Just as mulberry juice stains the hands, so sin stains the heart. And God was able to see that which was imprinted upon the heart of Cain as easily as mortal man can see that which is smeared upon the hands.

The sages say that God tested the wine-bottles of Adam and of Cain and found them both to be full of vinegar. This is their way of stating that God gave both these men a chance to do the manly thing, to acknowledge their sin and confess their guilt but in each case the opportunity was passed by. To Adam, God said, "Why did you eat of the fruit of the Tree?" Instead of admitting his guilt, Adam replied, "That Woman You gave me made me do it." To Cain, God said, "Where is your brother Abel?" Instead of telling the truth, Cain gave God an evasive answer, saying "Am I my brother's keeper?"

Then God said to Cain: "The voice of the blood of your brother is crying out to Me from the ground. How very naive you are, Cain. You actually believed that it would be possible to conceal this foul deed from Me. You remind me of another young man who once lived in another of My worlds. You know, of course, that I made and destroyed many worlds before creating this one. Well, as I was saying, this young man entered the pasture of his neighbor, picked up a young goat, threw it over his shoulder, and started to walk off with it. Just then the owner of the goat happened to come along. 'What's that you're carrying on your shoulder?' demanded the owner. 'Nothing,' replied the brazen poacher. To which the owner responded, 'That "nothing" is letting out some very loud and plaintive bleats.' Is there no limit to your impertinence and folly?"

"O Master of the universe," said Cain, "You must have speedy informers who delight in reporting to You the sins committed by human beings. My father and mother, who are right here on earth with me, do not yet know that I have killed Abel. And You, Who live so far away and have so many creatures to supervise, how is it that You already know?"

"You fool," replied God. "Did you not say just a few moments ago that I am the Guardian of all creatures and the Keeper of everything that lives? I sustain the whole universe and yet I am aware of every commandment of Mine which is obeyed and of every law of Mine that is broken."

"You bear the whole world and my sin You are not able to bear! Then the wrong which I have done must, indeed, be a grievous one."

"It certainly is. Anyone who wilfully destroys one human being whom I have created I shall hold as heavily accountable as though he had destroyed all of Creation. You have not killed just one man. You have killed millions and billions of people, all the unnumbered generations of the descendants of your brother who were yet to be. Only one voice is pleading with Me to be understanding and merciful. It is the voice of your brother Abel. He loved you in life and, even in death, he still seeks to protect you. You wicked man, why have you done this? You have murdered not only your blood-brother but also the one person in the world who truly loved you."

"I do not believe that he truly loved me. I admit that I was not able to read what was in his heart. I judged him only by his actions. And, from his actions, he seemed to be my enemy. Therefore I killed him.

"And why are You speaking to me in such a harsh tone? How was I to know that murder is such a heinous offense? The only creature I ever saw killed was the unicorn my father offered You as a sacrifice. The death of that animal seemed to please You. How was I to comprehend that You would show any more concern over the death of a man than You had shown when the unicorn was slaughtered? How was I to guess that the killing of my brother would make You so unhappy? And who ever told me that, if I were to beat him, he would die? For all You know, I never intended to kill him. I just meant to give him a sound thrashing.

"And, furthermore, is it not because of my father's sin that death came into the world? If my father had not sinned, I should never have been able to murder my brother. Why don't You punish my father for what I have done? He is the real cause of this crime, not I. After all, Abel was trespassing on my property. I was merely seeking to protect that which was lawfully and rightfully mine. Why should I be punished for putting into effect a policy which You Yourself decreed for the human race?

"To be perfectly candid, O Master, I do not believe that either my father or myself is nearly as responsible for Abel's death as You are. When did You ever tell me that I must be concerned about my brother's welfare? And how did this whole business get started? Who was it that made me jealous and angry by favoring Abel's offering and rejecting mine? Who was it that created the Evil Inclination which kept on tormenting me until, in desperation, I killed my brother? If one were to analyze this matter logically and dispassionately, he might very well come to the conclusion that the master-criminal in this unfortunate situation is not my father nor myself but You!"

The clarity and vehemence with which Cain presented his case took God somewhat aback. Such self-righteousness, such rebelliousness, such an utter lack of any feeling of guilt, He had not anticipated. God's reaction might, perhaps, have been more stern and uncompromising had it not been for the soul of Abel which made a strong plea in Cain's behalf.

"What Cain has said, O Master, makes good sense. You could have stopped the fight, if You had wanted to, before it was too late. Why did You not stop it? You certainly cannot deny that You are at least partially to blame for what has happened."

The sages say that Abel's argument was well-nigh unanswerable. The fight between Cain and Abel may be compared to that waged between two gladiators who were wrestling before their king. If the king had desired to prevent them from hurting each other, he could have stopped the match at any point. But the king had no desire to stop the match. He was interested only in its outcome. Therefore, the match continued until one gladiator prevailed against the other and killed him. One must grant that the king was quite directly responsible for the death of his wrestler.

How did God answer these charges? He said: "All of your arguments are very logical and very sensible. It is self-evident that I could easily have created a world of peace and harmony, a world without problems or conflict, if I had wished to do so. But this was not My wish nor My intention. I deliberately fashioned a world in which there would be both good and evil. And I deliberately placed in Man's keeping the power to choose between the two. If Man's life is not to be for him a meaningless moment between two eternities, if it is to be a challenging, stirring, satisfying experience, Man must be prepared to accept the responsibility of choice which I have given him. He must be ready to bear the consequences of his thoughts and actions. Humanity will not be able to escape from this Divinely imposed obligation by attempting to pin on Me the blame for its misdeeds.

"Then, too, Man must learn as quickly as possible that he lives neither for himself nor by himself. The individual in and of himself counts for nothing. It is only as the individual contributes to and draws from the life of the community that his existence takes on importance and significance. The individual's appearance on the stage of the world is but for a moment but the community's life goes on and on. Every deed of the individual must be considered in the light of its effect upon the community as well as upon the doer.

"Many situations will arise in which the murder of one individual by another will seem quite justifiable. One man will kill another because the other has stolen his cow or his horse or his wife. One woman will kill another because the other has taken from her a place by the fire or a golden ring or, perhaps, her husband. If individuals are to be permitted to commit murder every time one of them is seriously wronged, life on earth will be very hazardous, if not completely impossible. No one will be able to dwell with his fellow-men in peace and in safety. The good earth will not be cultivated. Houses will not be built. New communities will not be established. Every one will be on the move continually. Distrust and suspicion will be the dominant characteristics of human relationships.

"A society resting on such an insecure psychological foundation could not endure. Therefore, unauthorized and illegal murder will be prohibited. Murder, if it is to occur at all, will be socially regulated and controlled. Socially approved homicide will be limited to one of two situations: One, whenever an individual threatens or seems to threaten the welfare of those around him, society will take unto itself the right to put that individual to death in a manner which will be known as 'the due process of law.' And two, whenever one nation becomes a menace or seems to become a menace to another nation or to the world at large, many idealistic individuals, bearing no grudge against any other equally idealistic individuals but owing faithful allegiance to the wayward nation or to its noble enemies, will try to outdo each other in exterminating those on the other side systematically and scientifically in an atmosphere of hate and lies, which will be justified on both sides through the use of high-sounding words, ringing phrases, and learned treatises.

"As far as I the Lord your God am concerned, murder under whatever guise, for whatever reason, and through whatever process, legal or illegal, will always be regarded as murder and punished by Me as such. Society, taking a short-range view, will forfeit the life of that individual who fails to conform to its laws. And I, taking a long-range view, will forfeit the life of that nation or of that social system which fails to conform to My laws. The rule which I have stated to Cain applies to him and to all mankind now and for all time to come: Anyone who wilfully destroys one human being whom I have created I shall hold as heavily accountable as though he had destroyed all of Creation."

XII.   SOME ADDITIONAL
OBSERVATIONS

When Cain killed Abel, he found himself in conflict with one of the truly fundamental laws of the universe. This law, stated in its simplest form, is: God always inclines toward the side of the persecuted. Not just normally or usually but always. Of course, this is not made clear immediately to him who is being persecuted nor to those who are persecuting him nor to those who are watching him being persecuted. In fact, quite often the persecuted one has the feeling that he has been abandoned by God and by all mankind. From many an uncharted grave, individuals who have been done to death by lynching, pogrom, starvation, slavery, and other malignant manifestations of man's hatred for man would vigorously deny the validity of this law, if it were in their power to do so.

Nevertheless, there it is, in our law and in our tradition: God is always on the side of the persecuted and never on the side of the persecutor. God is always with him who is pursued and never with him who is the pursuer. God is always beside him who is hated and never with him who hates. Abel was hated by Cain but God was with Abel. Genesis 4:4, "And God looked with favor upon Abel." Noah was reviled by his generation but God saved only Noah. Genesis 7:1, "For you are the only good man that I have been able to find in this generation." When Abraham fled from Nimrod, God rescued him. Nehemiah 9:7, "Thou art the God Who chose Abraham and brought him forth from Ur Kasdim." The

(79)

Philistines drove Isaac away but God did not desert him. Genesis 26:28, "And the Philistines said, 'Now we are certain that God is with you.' " Jacob fled before Esau but God chose Jacob. Psalm 135:4, "For God has chosen Jacob as His own." Joseph was rejected by his brothers but God stood by Joseph. Psalm 81:6, "Joseph is the symbol of God's faithfulness to Man." The chariots of Pharaoh pressed in upon the people of Moses but God preserved them. Psalm 106:23, "Moses, His chosen one, stood in the breach before Him to turn back His wrath from destruction." Saul the king sought to destroy David the youthful musician but God was with the youth. Psalm 78:70, "He selected David as His servant." And the nations in hatred have driven Israel from one end of the world to the other but God has never permitted the bearer of His message to perish. Deuteronomy 14:2, "For you are a people consecrated to the Lord your God and, from all the peoples which are upon the face of the earth, God has chosen you to be His very own."

The sages say: This same principle was applied in the selection of animals that were considered worthy of being offered to God as a sacrifice. The ox flees before the lion. The goat flees before the leopard. The sheep flees before the wolf. Despite the strength of the lion, the speed of the leopard, and the bravery of the wolf, none of these pursuing animals was ever placed upon a sacrificial altar. But of the pursued, it is written, Leviticus 22:27, "An ox or a sheep or a goat . . . may be used for an offering made by fire unto the Lord."

The sages say further: Whether it be one righteous man who is trying to cause trouble for another righteous man or a wicked man who is trying to cause trouble for a righteous man or a wicked man who is trying to cause trouble for another wicked man, God is always on the side of the tormented one. Yes, even when a righteous man is trying to cause trouble for a wicked man, God is quite likely to aid the wicked one if the motives of the righteous man are not wholly pure. For,

as the Psalmist says, Psalm 145:9, "God's tender mercies
are upon all His works," which include the wicked as well
as the righteous; and it is not seemly for a righteous man to
be overly diligent in exacting punishment.

The essence of the matter is: The reactions of Man are not the
reactions of God nor are the methods of Man those of his Creator. Man's reactions and methods are conditioned by the fact
that today he is here and tomorrow he is gone, never to
return. God's reactions and methods are conditioned by the
fact that He has all of eternity in which to work out and to
make known His decisions and His judgments. Let not mortal
Man, in stupid haste, condemn the seeming unrighteousness
of deathless God. But let Man be ever aware that he who,
with hate in his heart, hunts down any other earthly being
brings in upon himself and upon generations to come the
calculated reactions of a Deity Whose law it is that love will
always be answered with Love and hate will be requited with
Hate. . . .

The sages attach great importance to the fact that the Hebrew
text of the Bible states that God said to Cain, "The voice
of the *bloods* of your brother is crying out unto Me from
the ground." The voice of the bloods, i.e., the voices not
only of Abel but of all the generations of his descendants
who, because of the murder, will never be born.

Murder is the most terrible of all crimes because it is so final
and so irrevocable. There is no way in which it may ever
be undone or properly atoned. In a case in which only property is involved, it is possible to make adequate restitution,
either by restoring the property or paying its equivalent in
money or other material goods. But all the money and property in the world cannot restore one life nor can it pay for
the damage done to other lives when a life has been wrongfully taken. In a case which involves only material goods,
the voice of the wronged one may be hushed by stuffing his
mouth with money. But at any place in the world where
murder has been committed, the voice of the murdered one
continues to cry out from the ground forever.

Therefore Judaism is most careful in defining the circumstances under which legal murder, i.e., capital punishment, may be permitted. In practice, Jews are opposed to the death penalty for any and all crimes. Jews are opposed to the taking of human life under any and all circumstances. If the world were to be compelled to use only a willing religious Jew as its official executioner, no one would ever be shot, hanged, gassed, or electrocuted. However, Jews are compelled to concede that there are some crimes for which, theoretically at least, a culprit deserves to be executed. Anyone who commits a carefully planned, deliberate murder deserves to die. After all, does the Bible not say, Exodus 21:23, "A life for a life"?

But Jewish law is religious law. Being religious law, it is a law based on faith, faith that God will surely and wisely punish the guilty, whether or not he is punished by Man. Therefore, Man, in attempting to administer the law, must be extremely sure that, in his effort to punish the guilty, he never wrongs the innocent. In fact, in any legal action, the judges must be more concerned about protecting the innocent than they are about punishing the guilty.

In accordance with this premise, Jewish law establishes the following procedure for trying a person accused of murder:

There are no lawyers and no jury. The trial is conducted by a Sanhedrin or court of twenty-three well-trained judges, who vigorously cross-examine the defendant and the witnesses, consider the evidence, and arrive at a suitable verdict.

Capital punishment is not permitted for any crime which was not witnessed by two or more reliable witnesses. The following classes of persons are excluded from serving as reliable witnesses in a murder case:

1) Any person who is related by blood or marriage to either the murdered person, the defendant, or any of the other qualified witnesses.
2) Women, minors, and slaves.
3) Anyone who does not observe daily the principles and

(82)

practices of the Jewish religion, i.e., all non-Jews and irreligious **Jews.**

4) Anyone of bad reputation, anyone previously convicted of perjury, tax collectors, professional gamblers, and black marketeers.

5) Deaf mutes, the blind, and the insane.

6) Anyone who has been paid to testify.

Even if the criminal confesses voluntarily, capital punishment may not be administered unless a minimum of two acceptable witnesses observed the commission of the crime.

If the murder-instrument is one which ordinarily would not cause death or if the health of the murdered person was such that there is some doubt as to whether a robust person would have succumbed to the same blow or blows, the death penalty may not be imposed.

In a case involving the possibility of capital punishment, all circumstantial evidence is ruled out completely. With regard to this point, the Talmud states: "If you see one man pursue another into a deserted house and you run into the house after them and you find one standing with a knife in his hand and blood is dripping from the knife and the other is lying on the ground dead, having been stabbed to death, so far as the legal value of your testimony is concerned, you have seen absolutely nothing!"

The Talmud also says: "How do judges impress upon witnesses in a capital case the seriousness of the matter? They gather the witnesses together and warn them that they shall not offer any testimony which is based on guess-work or hearsay. They tell them that they will be cross-examined severely because capital cases are much more carefully handled than cases involving only money-damages. In a damage suit, a man pays a fine and the case is concluded, but the decision in a capital case affects the life of the accused and the lives of all his descendants from now to the end of the world. For so it was in the case of Cain's murder of his brother. God said, 'The voice of the bloods of your brother is crying out

unto Me,' i.e., the blood of Abel and of all his descendants."
It is easy now to understand why the Talmud maintains that any
Sanhedrin which sentences just one person to death every
seven years is known as a "bloody Sanhedrin." Eleazar ben
Azariah adds that he would apply this term to any Sanhedrin
which orders the execution of a single criminal even once in
every seventy years.

THE SHARP EXCHANGE between God and Cain continued for many days. God did not want to be accused of being hasty in judgment or of being vindictive in His reaction to wrong-doing. While the trial was in progress, many beasts and birds gathered and listened intently to the dramatic debate. Among those present was the Serpent, already demoted to the lowest rank in the animal kingdom and already fashioned and garbed in the ugliest of forms and colors.

When both Cain and God had made their final statements, the Dog came forward and began to bark: "I have just come from the grave of Abel. With these paws I helped dig the hole which is now my master's final resting-place. With these eyes I witnessed the overwhelming grief of Abel's father and mother. With these ears I heard them ask You, O Lord, what shall be said and done to a son who has murdered his only brother. Their lives have been ruined, their fondest hopes dashed to pieces, their ambitions crushed.

"Think for a moment of what this foul deed means not only to Abel's fine parents but also to the unnumbered host of his descendants who will now never see and feel life. Shall the murderer be permitted to breed more and more genera-tions of evil ones, while the name of his fallen victim is gradu-ally wiped away by the passing centuries?

"And what does the future now hold for us, the more humble of the creatures of earth? Abel was more than our master. He was our friend. He loved us. He nurtured us. He restored us to health when we were sick. When we were hungry, he fed us, and when we were thirsty, he gave us water. Without the strong hand of our leader to guide us, how shall we be able to maintain life and health and strength?

"Cain must die! His fate must serve as an eternal warning to those who are tempted to disobey the laws of God and to disturb the ways of beasts and men. The murder of Abel, the grief of his parents, the annihilation of the unborn, the helplessness of the herds and the flocks, all these must be avenged. I demand that Cain be put to death. Cain must die!"

Then all the other animals and birds, the lion, the fox, and the Serpent, the eagle, the owl, and the dove, began to shout in unison, loudly and insistently: "Cain must die! Cain must die!"

The noisy din was silenced by the voice of the Lord. "Stop your howling, O animals, and cease your twittering, O birds. Cain is not going to be put to death because of the crime which he has committed. It would not be fair to subject him to a penalty which has not yet been established either by law or precedent. Nor would it be fair, at this early stage of the world's development, to put Adam and Eve through the agonizing experience of thinking that the human race, just newly begun, is so soon to become extinct. Cain cannot be judged or punished in the same way that future murderers will be judged and punished. Since no one has ever been murdered before, Cain may rightfully claim that he was unaware of the heinousness of his crime. Since the guiding light of the Torah has not yet been made available to mankind, Cain cannot be expected to understand fully man's obligation to man. In later days, the law-makers of Judaism will decree that no one guilty of murder may be executed unless the crime has been committed in the presence of two or more reliable witnesses. Let us be at least as merciful as they. Let us never, my furred and feathered friends, bring the non-human down to the level of the inhuman. May the creatures of the forest and jungle ever be able to say to those who walk on only two feet: 'Look at us, you brainy fools, and learn how to live and to let live!'

"In future years, one who commits premeditated, deliberate murder will either be executed or imprisoned. One who kills another unintentionally will be condemned to perpetual exile. Even though Cain killed Abel with thoroughly planned malice, I intend to impose upon him the less severe sentence of the accidental murderer. Exile seems to be a quite appropriate punishment in this instance for a number of reasons, which shall be enumerated as I pronounce sentence:

"Cain, having carefully considered all the factors involved in the case of Humanity versus Cain, I do sentence you to wander around the Earth continually for the rest of your natural life.

"Because you wished to own the whole world, you shall own none of it. Power flees desperately from those who pursue her too ardently. Proverbs 28:22, 'He that has an evil eye hastens after riches and knows not that want will come upon him.' Everyone who seeks to obtain something which is not meant for him not only fails to get that which he seeks but also loses much, if not all, of what he already has. So it was with the Serpent and so it is with Cain.

"Because you were so anxious to get Abel out of the way

in order that you might not be disturbed by his presence, you shall be avoided henceforth by both man and beast. Only your immediate family will be permitted to associate with you. No place on earth will want you as an inhabitant. You shall never again have continuing peace of mind or bodily ease. A fugitive and a wanderer shall you be for the remainder of your days.

"Because you would not permit Abel to rest upon your property but sarcastically told him to fly away like a bird and because you followed him relentlessly from place to place, you, too, shall never be permitted to rest in any one place for even a moment. Whenever and wherever you stop, the ground that is under you will start to quake and will continue to do so until you move to another spot.

"Thus, in your own time and throughout the generations, men will point to you as a vivid example of what happens to one who succumbs to the impulse to murder his fellow-man. The annals of human history will record that you were an evil man who suffered greatly because of his evil. Your name will be pronounced with scorn and with malediction."

The sages say that, because Cain was so avaricious, he was given the most severe punishment that an avaricious man can receive, i.e., he had to live as a vagrant on the estate where formerly he had been master. So it will be with anyone whose love of earthly wealth is greater than his love of his fellow-man. The sages say further that to be removed permanently from one's house and one's possessions is a punishment worse than death.

The Lord continued to speak. "The ground, too, shall be

punished because it tried to protect its master by swallowing the blood of Abel. It hoped, in this way, to conceal Cain's crime from Me. While loyalty is a commendable virtue, one must sometimes choose between two loyalties and decide which is the greater and the more uncompromising. One's obligation to the Supreme Commander always takes precedence over one's love for or responsibility to the subordinate authorities of Earth.

"The established order of the world shall be that, wherever murder is committed, the blood of the murdered one must remain on the surface of the ground as evidence that, on this spot, life has been wrongfully taken. To seek to protect a murderer is a false kind of humanitarianism, for it permits one who is a potential social menace to remain at large and such action may jeopardize the lives of innocent people.

"As a fit punishment for having been more faithful to Cain than to the God Who created him, the ground will not be permitted to work for or with Cain while he lives nor to receive his body when he dies. Never again will the earth be allowed to yield her increase to Cain. His career as a farmer is finished. His working partnership with the earth is dissolved."

Actually, it was Cain rather than the ground who was cursed by this decision. The ground would find many other human partners but Cain would never again be able to follow his beloved vocation.

There is no earthly tie more strong than that which binds the farmer to his land and no mental pain more agonizing than that which results from a farmer's being separated from his land. Ownership of land gives the farmer a feeling of security and well-being. A farmer without land is like a captain without a ship, a preacher without a pulpit, a soldier without a gun. Such a farmer is not only propertyless and occupationless. He is homeless, helpless, and hopeless. . . .

From that day to this, the ground has never opened her mouth unless God has commanded her to do so. One bitter lesson was enough. In later days, after Moses had led the children of Israel through the Red Sea and the Red Sea had drowned the pursuing Egyptian soldiers, a controversy arose between the Land and the Sea over the burial of these dead soldiers. The Sea was casting the Egyptian dead upon the Land and the Land was throwing them back into the Sea. The Sea said to the Land: "Receive back your army;" and the Land said to the Sea: "Keep to yourself those whom you have slain. When I voluntarily took within myself the blood of just one murdered man, God punished me. Now if I open my mouth to receive all these whom you have murdered, how much greater will be my punishment!" At that moment, God spoke and said, "O Land, you may take them this time. As recompense, I shall, on some future occasion, order an army which has been killed on land to be cast into the sea for burial." The Land was still not convinced. "O God," she said, "promise me by all that is Holy that, if I do this, You will not punish me." "I promise," said God. Whereupon the Land opened up her mouth and swallowed all the Egyptian dead.

XIV. CAIN REPENTS (SOMEWHAT) AND GOD RELENTS (SOMEWHAT)

AFTER GOD had announced His decision, He said to Cain, "Is there anything you would like to say to Me before I order your sentence to be put into effect?" "Let me have a few minutes to think this over," requested Cain. "Surely," God said.

While Cain was not truly repentant in the sense that he was genuinely sorry for or even ashamed of what he had done, he was finally beginning to realize that what he had done was wrong and that he would now be much better off if he had not done it. Yet it was difficult for him to believe that, in murdering Abel, he had committed a cardinal sin. One who murders another, he argued to himself, is sinning only against Man, which certainly does not put the sin in the same category with such sins as blasphemy and atheism, which are offenses against God.

Later on in Jewish history, the sages show how they feel about this point of view by decreeing that the three unpardonable human crimes are murder, incest, and idolatry. By so doing, the sages indicate that there are times when one who sins against another person or against society commits as serious an offense as one who sins against God.

As Cain gave further thought to the matter, he began to understand why murder is an almost unforgivable sin, because genuine forgiveness is really only possible where proper restitution is possible. In almost every crime except murder, one who repents is able to make some form of appropriate amends, but what may one give back to another after he has taken that other's life? Wealth? Property? Labor? Good deeds? Of what avail will any of these be to the dead? They may give comfort to the living. They may cause the living to try to forgive and forget. But of what avail are they to him who is dead? All the promises and tears in the world will not bring the dead back to life.

Knowing that God was well aware that he was not truly repentant and knowing also that he really felt more sorry for himself than he did for either his bad conduct or his dead brother, Cain realized that it was useless to ask God to forgive him or even to mitigate his punishment. But he was afraid that, from this time forth, the creatures of the world would be infuriated against him so that, wherever he would go, some of them would try to kill him. Therefore, Cain decided it would be wise for him to ask God not for Divine forgiveness but for Divine protection. And that is what he did.

"O all-righteous Master, You have decided well and I accept Your decision without complaint. However, I feel that, unless I get help from You, the punishment which You have decreed for me will not be carried out in the way that You intend. You have said that You are sentencing me to perpetual exile, which is the punishment for unintentional murder, rather than putting me to death, which henceforth will be the punishment for intentional murder. This seems fair because it is, in a way, the same punishment that You decreed for my father for a similar misdeed. When Adam unknowingly brought death into the world, You drove him out of the Garden of Eden. Now that I have sinned in like manner by committing murder when I was not completely aware of the gravity of my offense, I, too, am to be punished by being exiled. However, it is quite apparent that I am being punished much more severely than was my father. I am quite willing to admit that mine was, indeed, a greater crime; but I feel that I am being placed in greater jeopardy than You intended. Many who meet me will try to kill me because they will feel that such an act will be pleasing to You. You must give me some kind of protection which will indicate that it is Your wish that I remain alive and unharmed, so that I may be shielded against those who are overly zealous."

God was deeply impressed by the good sense and sound logic of Cain's words. In fact, He was so deeply impressed by Cain's conciliatory attitude that He decided to remit a portion of his punishment. Originally He had determined that Cain was not only to be obliged to be on the move continually from place to place but also that, whenever he stopped at one spot, the earth was to quake under him and he was to keep moving around on the spot where he stood. As a result of Cain's fine words, God decided to annul the last part of the sentence, i.e., when Cain would stop at one place, the ground under him would start to quake and would continue to do so as long as Cain remained there but Cain himself would not be required to keep moving in place. Therefore, after he had adjusted himself to this new way of living, Cain would be able to get some rest each night and periodically throughout each day.

When God informed His Heavenly Family that He had

granted this concession to Cain, the Angel of the Sabbath stepped forward. As she had pleaded previously that Adam must not be forced to violate the spirit of the Sabbath, so now she advanced the same argument in behalf of Cain. "O Universal Ruler," she cried, "it certainly cannot be Your intention to have the punishment of Cain go on even during the Sabbath Day. Is Cain to continue to move about when all else that lives is at rest? If Cain halts on the Sabbath, is the ground beneath him to continue to quake so that the peace and quiet of his resting-place will be disturbed seriously throughout the Day dedicated to peace and quiet? Are the duties and obligations of the Sabbath, its blessings and its benefits, for all mankind, the good and evil, for those in the prison as well as those in the palace, or are its privileges and its responsibilities to be reserved only for the chosen few whom You regard as the elect among men? O Holy One, I ask You to make of the Sabbath a truly universal day of rest for all the animal world, for man and for beast, by decreeing that the punishment of even the most wicked shall be suspended on this Day." God listened and approved. Thus Cain gained another important diminution of his punishment. He was to be allowed the peace of mind and rest of body which come to all the world each week on the holy Sabbath Day.

God next took up the matter of finding means of protecting Cain against those who might seek to kill him as he wandered about.

Some may wonder why God bothered Himself with such a trivial matter as the preservation of the life of such a miserable, worthless individual. It has already been pointed out that one reason was that God wanted Cain to serve as a living warning to all others who might be tempted to murder their fellow-creatures. The sages interpret the Divine concern in yet another way. It is proof to them that God was really very pleased with the manner in which Cain comported himself after sentence had been pronounced. God believed that Cain had come to the realization that it is neither wise nor possible for any individual to turn his life in a direction that runs counter to the pattern and laws of the universe. So he had decided to make a determined effort to adjust himself to God's way of thinking and doing. Therefore, God granted Cain the same guidance and protection which He gives to anyone who strives to live in accordance with His Divine principles. . . .

The sages say that, in some ways, God manages His relationships with Man in much the same manner as earthly governments handle their constituents. The relationship between God and Man is largely a matter of law. God's laws, like the essential statutes of earth, are well-known and easy to understand. Obey these laws and life goes well; disregard them and accept the consequences. Although many may not like to admit it, the manner in which God decides our fate is just about as professional and impersonal as the way in which earthly governments control their citizens. We hear talk sometimes of a Personal God who watches Personally over every action of every creature of earth. If this is interpreted too literally, it becomes a very nonsensical and egotistical concept. When we do what God wants us to do, when we obey His laws, He watches over us, i.e., all goes well with us and we are able to develop our capabilities to their utmost limits. When we cease to live in accordance with His laws, i.e., do that which is evil in His sight, He stops protecting us, i.e., we endure the agonies of frustration, failure, and bitterness of mind and body.

We must always keep this in mind: Man has not brought God to Earth to serve us. God has put Man here to serve Him.

When one recognizes and understands the difference between using God as a crutch and making oneself an humble instrument of His purpose and His will, he abandons the false theological ideas which deify Man and proceeds onward and upward, ennobled by the most blessed of hopes and ambitions, the determination to serve God worthily.

Cain had convinced God that he was determined to become a worthy citizen of God's spiritual kingdom. The punishment which God had imposed on Cain would make it necessary for him to travel in strange, sometimes hostile, territory. Therefore, employing a device used by earthly rulers and governments, God gave Cain a highly respected and an easily identifiable passport, a means of indicating that Cain was under God's protection and that he was entitled to wander about the earth without undue interference from the various inhabitants thereof.

THE PASSPORT which God gave to Cain did not look like the passports of modern times. It was not a multitude of words written down in a little book, together with an assortment of photographs, endorsements, and signatures. God printed the words of His passport on Cain's body, on nature, and on the minds of Cain's contemporaries. The passport was divided into six sections, which, when added together, were certain to put the fear of God into the hearts of all who might come in contact with Cain.

These six sections consisted of:

1) A sign on Cain's forehead
2) A sign on Cain's arm
3) A skin disease
4) A miracle of nature
5) An animal
        and
6) A Divine promise and threat.

Let us describe each of them and consider their meanings.

1) *The sign on Cain's forehead*

The sign which God placed on the forehead of Cain was the horn of a unicorn.

This is the opinion of the majority of the sages but not of all of them. The Biblical commentator Maharshal says that God carved two Hebrew letters on Cain's forehead, a Tav to represent the Hebrew word "tich'ye" meaning "you shall live" and a Heh to represent the Hebrew word for God and to indicate that this was a message from the Almighty. Rashi says that God burned the shape of a pig into Cain's forehead because everyone, human and animal, shies away at the sight of a pig. Ibn Ezra says that there may have been no visible sign on Cain but God may have strengthened his heart so that he feared nothing and so that all feared him. None of these statements represents the majority opinion. The majority opinion is that the horn of a unicorn protruded from the forehead of Cain.

God selected the sign of the unicorn for a number of reasons. In the first place, this gave Cain a weapon with which to defend himself if any animal should attack him. Since at this time there were no human beings in the world beside his own immediate family, the only creatures whom he really needed to fear were the animals. It will be remembered that, at the trial, the animals had demanded of God that Cain be put to death. Therefore he had genuine reason to fear them. In the second place, the use of the unicorn's horn was symbolic. Just as the first animal to be sacrificed to God was a unicorn, so now the unicorn's horn was to be a sign that henceforth Cain's life was to be dedicated to God and was subject to His will. The horn is shaped like the Hebrew letter Vav, which is one of the letters in the Hebrew name for God. No matter from what direction or angle one views the Vav, its appearance is unchanged. Therefore, the Vav may be said to represent the eternality and unchangeability of the Divine element in human life. Like his father, Cain had formerly entertained heretical opinions with regard to God and, like his father, Cain had become convinced of the error of his earlier theological views. As was mentioned in connection with Adam, the pointing of the horn toward the heavens was an indication that Cain's thoughts were now turned in the right direction. Finally, from a very practical point of view, the horn was a sign that would be easy to recognize at a great distance and would give advance warning of Cain's approach.

2) *The sign on Cain's arm*

God branded the Hebrew letter Tav on Cain's arm.

The letter Tav was selected because it is the first letter of the Hebrew words meaning "Thou shalt live" and "Thou shalt die"; it is the last letter of God's seal, which is the Hebrew word "emes" meaning "truth"; and it is the first letter of the word "Torah" and the last letter of the Hebrew alphabet and thus signifies that one should study Torah from the cradle to the grave.

3) *The skin disease*

Cain was smitten with a skin disease which caused his whole body to glisten. Spots appeared on his skin which were brightly white and which sparkled like snow.

The sages believe that the skin disease from which Cain suffered was leprosy.

People are afflicted with leprosy, says Rabbi Judah ha-Levi son of Rabbi Shalom, for eleven crimes: Murder, incest, cursing God, lying, pride, stealing, deceit, trespassing, false oaths, profaning God's name, and idolatry. Rabbi Isaac adds: For possessing an evil eye. Others add: For giving too broad an interpretation to the words of the Torah.

What does Rabbi Isaac mean by "possessing an evil eye?" He means one who is narrow-visioned, one who is not concerned about the welfare of his neighbor. His neighbor says to him, "Lend me a little wheat." He says, "I have neither wheat nor barley nor figs to lend." His neighbor's wife says to him, "I should like to borrow a sieve and a basket." He replies, "I have nothing to lend." What does God do? He sends the plague of leprosy on that man's house and out come all his stores of food and all his utensils. Then everybody who passes by can see that this man had an abundance of everything to lend if he had been willing to do so. Cursed with leprosy shall be any house which has accursed owners.

The sages are wrong. Cain's symptoms, as listed by the Midrash, are not those of leprosy. Also, contrary to the statements in the thirteenth chapter of the Biblical book of Leviticus and in the Midrash, it is not possible for a house to have leprosy. The Bible and Midrash seem to be referring to a type of fungus which can be acquired both by a dwelling and a human being. Whatever that particular disease may have been or may be, it caused Cain much discomfort, it made his skin glisten, and it served as an added deterrent for those who might have wished to get close to Cain in order to do him harm.

4) *The miracle of nature*

The sun shone continually on Cain, both by day and by night.

The sun is a symbol of peace. It served as a sign that God wanted everyone, both human and animal, to let Cain live in peace.

The sun is a symbol of light. Criminals shun the light and skulk about in the dark. Cain lived in the sunlight so that it would

be known that he was not an habitual criminal. He had committed a terrible wrong and he was being punished for it.
But he had no intention of repeating his mistake. His life
was an open book. Whoever chanced to pass by him, at any
hour of the day or the night, could see what he was doing.
During the remainder of his life, he was never to have one
moment of complete privacy.

The sun is a symbol of protection. One would think that living
in the sunlight would have made Cain easier to find and to
kill. But the only real enemies that Cain had were the wild
animals. Wild beasts fear the sun and have much less power
over Man in the light than in the dark. Thus the sun was an
important factor in protecting Cain from danger.

The sun is a symbol of Divine comfort. Cain feared that, once
he began his years of wandering, he would be neglected and
forgotten by God and Man. The rays of the sun were a
constant assurance to him that he had not been forgotten and
that God was with him in the hours of darkness as well as
in the hours of light.

5) *The animal*

The dog which had been Abel's constant companion and
which had helped Abel to tend his flocks was given to Cain
as a servant, guard, and guide. The dog was commanded to
make sure that no animal or human being ever attacked his
new master. Since the dog had been the most vehement
among the animals demanding the death penalty for Cain,
God reasoned that he would be the ideal watchman over Cain.
When the other animals would see him guarding Cain, they
would say: "Why should we continue to harbor resentment
against Cain for killing Abel? Abel's closest animal friend
and most loyal helper, the Dog, has made his peace with

Cain and is now working with him. Why should we not do likewise?" Cain always wandered in whatever direction the dog wanted to go, because he knew that the dog was sent from God and he regarded the desires of the dog as the will of God.

6) *The Divine promise and threat*

God said, "I shall continue to protect Cain for seven generations. During this period of time, if anyone shall kill him or even attempt to kill him, I shall avenge such a murder or such an attempt at murder seven-fold." This declaration was addressed primarily to the animals and birds, since none of the human beings then in the world had given any indication of desiring the death of Cain. None of them would have wanted to take on himself or herself the possible responsibility of causing the extinction of the human race.

From God's statement we learn that, in His sight, an assault
with intent to kill is just as serious a crime as actual murder.
According to Jewish law, an earthly court may not punish
a person for intent to commit murder. In order to be subject
to the penalty for murder, a person must actually commit a
murder. However, Jewish law takes it for granted that, even
though murderous intent cannot and will not be punished by
an earthly court, God will, in His own good time, exact
a fitting punishment from any person guilty of assault with
intent to murder. . . .

* * * * * * *

There is disagreement among the sages as to whether or not Cain
really had all six of these protective devices. Some say that he
had the sign on his forehead but not on his arm and vice

versa. Some insist that he was not blessed with perpetual sunlight but that the disease which he had made him appear to emit continual rays of light. Some maintain that he was not accompanied by Abel's dog during his wanderings. There is unanimous agreement that God promised to shield Cain for seven generations and threatened to punish severely anyone who would hurt him during that length of time. None of the sages seems to believe that Cain was protected in less than three ways and there are some who seem to accept without reservation the necessity for and the existence of all six means of protection.

"YOUR TRIAL has been completed, sentence has been pronounced, and the necessary safeguards have been placed about your person," said God to Cain. "Your years of wandering will now begin. You will go forth from here toward the East and there you will spend the remainder of your days."

According to Biblical law, anyone guilty of unintentional murder is exiled toward the East. Adam, after being forced to leave the Garden of Eden, was directed to move eastward because he was considered a murderer. Although he had not killed anyone deliberately or directly, he had, through his disobedience of God's command, brought death into the world and he was, in consequence, guilty of murder on such a wholesale scale that the most bloody war-lord or tyrant can never hope to match his record. In later days, cities of refuge were established east of the land of Israel for those who had committed murder accidentally. The Bible states, Deuteronomy 4:41-42, "Then Moses set aside three cities beyond the Jordan toward the rising of the sun as places to which one who has committed murder accidentally may flee and there he may live."

So Cain went away from the place where he had been

tried. He had gone only a short distance when he was greeted
by Adam, who had been waiting for the outcome of the trial
as patiently and calmly as a father could under such circumstances. What a strange and bitter meeting it was for both
men! Adam, bereft of one son, delighted that the life of his
other son had been spared, and yet seeing that other son
standing before him in such a pitiable condition: a long horn
growing from his forehead, his body covered with sores, the
ground quaking beneath him, and being led about by a
dog! Cain, glad that he was still alive; but what an ordeal
for one who had been so proud, so ambitious, so powerful,
to have to meet his father in such a sorry state!

"Well, my son, how did it go?" asked Adam. "Not so well,"
replied Cain, "but it would have gone much worse if I had
not finally admitted that He was right and I was wrong. Because of this improvement in my attitude, God remitted part
of my punishment. He has given me permission to rest completely one day in every seven. As you can see, He has
changed my appearance in order to protect me against those
who might seek to kill me." "Would that I had known, when
God was judging me for my sin," commented Adam, "how
much one's punishment may be mitigated by proper repentance! It is wise to confess one's sins before God."

The Jews agree with Adam. On each Sabbath Day, they say in
their prayers: "Tov l'hodos Ladonai. It is wise to confess
one's sins before God."
Does God attach greater importance to the confession of a repentant sinner than he does to the prayer of a righteous man
who is in difficulty? Rabbi Judah ben Chiyya says: Repentance accomplishes only half as much as the prayers of the

(105)

righteous. Rabbi Joshua ben Levi says: The prayers of the righteous accomplish only half as much as genuine repentance.

Another answer to this theological question, an answer which is a fine formulation of the Jewish attitude with regard to prayer in general, is given by Rabbi Eliezer: God places a great value on any sincere prayer, no matter from whom or from where it comes. However, one must recognize prayer for what it is and realize what it can accomplish and what it can not accomplish. Prayer is Man's pledge to attempt to perfect himself before God. Prayer, no matter how sincere, will never yield a pledge from God to give Man everything that he wants. No prayer goes unanswered; but the measure of the answer is determined by the integrity and unselfishness of him who utters the prayer.

Cain next presented himself to his sorrowing mother, wife, and sister-in-law in order to acquaint them with the Divine decision. He promised his wife that he would spend as many Sabbaths with her as his canine guide would permit. Then he took leave of his relatives and set off toward the East to begin a seemingly endless journey to Nowhere, a journey that would go on and on year after year after year.

The life of Cain from this time forward proceeded according to a very fixed pattern. For six days out of every seven, he was in continual pain and torment and constantly on the move. Wherever he wandered, he was an object of contempt, derision, and hate. When he would stop to rest for a while, the ground under him would begin to quake. The animals in the neighborhood would gather together and ask each other: "Who is this creature who is causing us this trouble?" A knowing one would answer: "This is the man Cain who killed his brother. God has decreed that he shall wander about as an exile for the rest of his life." There would always be some well-meaning but uninformed beast who would then boldly propose that Cain be killed and eaten. The animals would congregate around Cain in a threatening manner, while his Dog barked and snarled at them in order to try to make them disperse.

At this moment, Cain's eyes would fill with tears and he would feel helpless and afraid. But this mood of insecurity would soon pass. God's perpetual sunlight would assure him that all would be well and that he must not fear. Then Cain would pray, calmly and trustingly, Psalm 139:7-10: "Whither may I go from Thy spirit? Or whither shall I flee from Thy presence? If I ascend into the heavens, Thou art there; if I make my bed in the nether-world, behold, Thou art there. If I take the wings of the morning, and dwell in the uttermost parts of the sea, even there would Thy hand lead me, and Thy right hand would hold me."

After a while the animals would stop tormenting him, but they would order Cain to leave their territory immediately and not come back. This happened so often that Cain became convinced that God must have given some evil spirit the duty of stirring up the animals against him wherever he went. He never saw the spirit but he was sure that it must be about him somewhere.

At times he would try to till the soil in various parts of the territory which he covered but it was no use. Nothing except thorns and thistles grew on the land which he sought to cultivate. He was not able to provide any food for himself. He was compelled to subsist on the charity of his relatives and the wild berries, roots, and nuts which he was able to gather in the forests and fields. His was, indeed, a miserable existence.

However, Cain's life was not altogether devoid of material and spiritual happiness. He obtained periodic surcease from his troubles from two sources: the Sabbath and his family. Every seventh day, on Friday evening, as soon as three stars would appear in the sky, the horn would disappear from Cain's forehead, the sores would vanish from his body, the ground would cease to quake beneath him, and Cain would settle down to twenty-four hours of normal living. How he looked forward to the Sabbath, especially to those blessed Days of Rest which he was permitted to spend with his family.

At first, Cain was troubled by the thought that, because he had sinned, God would not permit him to have any children. Great was his joy when his wife became pregnant and gave birth to a son, Enoch. Even though he had lost all his own material possessions, Cain determined to devote every possible moment he could to providing his son with a material treasure and a monument that would stand forever. He would build a city and he would name the city after his son Enoch!

For the rest of his life, Cain labored at the building of this city. He could not work at this project for very many hours at a time, of course. Between short intervals of furious, painful, back-breaking work, there were long periods of aggravating, solitary wandering. And, of course, Cain was not permitted to live in any part of the city which he was building. He never finished the city nor even a small section of it; but it kept his mind feverishly occupied during his waking hours and spurred on the hope that he might be able to regain, through his son and his son's name, some of the heights of material power, glory, and fame which he himself had won and then lost.

Human nature is, indeed, a curious phenomenon. One would have thought that Cain's shattering experience and continuing ordeal would have eradicated thoughts of ambition and might from his mind entirely and permanently. But it was not so. He had suffered a severe set-back, but the thoughts were still there. In the Cain-mind, no matter what happens, they are always there and they never go away. The Cain-mind may at times become regretful but it never becomes saintly. The Cain-mind may sometimes ask, "Why did this happen to me?" and "What is the smallest amount of righteous living which I must endure in order to get back on my feet again?" but it will rarely be genuinely repentant and it will never completely change.

That is the way a thorough-going materialist is. He builds continually for his own selfish purposes. He never finishes building because he is never satisfied with what he has already built. If he has an edifice fifty stories high, he dreams of owning one a hundred stories high. If he has amassed a million dollars, he wants two million. When he reaches two million, he starts after three million. And so it goes. Even in sleep, his soul is not at rest. In his dreams, he grabs, schemes, robs. He is ever seeking for he knows not what. In the end, he dies as ignorant, as unhappy, and as dissatisfied as when he began. After he is gone, pot-bellied idlers feast upon that which he planted and built, that for which he struggled and sweated.

In the Hebrew alphabet, the letters of the word "awni," meaning "poor," are right next to the letters for the word "kesef," meaning "money," except that the sequence of the letters in one word, Ayin, Nun, Yod, is exactly the opposite of the sequence of the letters in the other word, Kaf, Samech, Feh. This teaches, say the sages, that he who seeks constantly after material wealth may achieve his objective but he will also achieve its opposite, poverty of mind and soul.

"And Cain named the city which he was building after his son, Enoch." What a monstrous conceit fills the mind of such a one as Cain! He will outwit the laws of the universe. He will die in the flesh but his power will live on through his children. His remembrance will be kept alive by bricks and stones. What a monstrous conceit! Hear this, you obstinate fool, you deluded offspring of the Serpent; listen to these words right out of the pages of the Bible, straight from the mouth of the Lord:

Psalm 49:17-18, 11-13

Fear not when a man gets rich,
When the splendor of his house increases;
For he will take nothing with him when he dies;
His splendor will not endure after him. . . .
Yea, wise men die;
But the fool and the brute also perish;
And they leave their wealth to others.
Their graves are their houses forever,
Their dwellings for one generation after another.
That man who seeks to perpetuate his name
Is as the ox, lacking understanding;
As the beast vanishes,
So shall he vanish,
Sayeth the Lord.

Cain's counterparts are present in every generation. Now and then, one is found who appears to retain a capability for spiritual comprehension and a desire for spiritual redemption.

If such a one should happen to read these pages, the rest of this chapter is meant for him:

This is the lot of mortal man:

Psalm 90:9-10, "The days of his years are three-score years and ten, or perhaps, by reason of strength, four-score years. They are a weird combination of travail and vanity. They fly by speedily and fade away. They come to an end as a tale that is told."

Fifty years more: All that is left of him who was rich and strong and well-formed is a small heap of dry bones.

Another hundred years: Idleness, carelessness, and indifference have eaten up his gold.

Add three hundred years: The houses he built have crumbled to dust; the name on his tombstone has worn away.

Add five hundred years: His family history has vanished from the pages of the books in the libraries.

Add one thousand years: No human mind knows and no human heart cares about the fact that there was once such a person as he.

O creature of dust, consider these things.

Creature of dust, realize what you are and before Whom you stand. Do not attempt to side-step the unavoidable, to hold back the inevitable, or to preserve the ephemeral. Deny your self. Forget your false hopes, your foolish dreams, your vain ambitions. Live for the happiness of your family and your neighbors *now*. Live for the welfare of your community and your nation *now*. Live on eternally through the laughter and the peace of a better world which you can begin to help to create *now, now, NOW!*

It will not be easy, O child of Cain. It will not be easy. Satan will be waiting to discourage you at every step of the way. To turn aside from self and to plunge into the struggle that stands between you and your soul's salvation is an experience which only the hardiest and the bravest may endure. But turn aside you will—if you want to love God; and turn aside you must—if you want God to love you.

XVII. SIX GENERATIONS PASS BY

Solomon wrote, Ecclesiastes 6:3, "If a man fathers a hundred children and lives many years and yet is never satisfied with what he has, and moreover does not receive a decent burial, I declare that the prematurely dead is better off than he." The sages say that the wise king was thinking of Cain.

Cain had a hundred children. He lived for many years. Because of his insatiable desire for material wealth and power, he murdered Abel. In consequence, he suffered bitter physical torment and wearied himself with ceaseless wandering.

Abel, prematurely dead, was better off lying in his grave than was Cain, the living fratricide. Abel, prematurely dead, occupies a more noble place in Jewish history and tradition than does Cain who lived many years and had a hundred children.

Cain did what he could to insure the perpetuation of the human species. However, the name of only one of his sons has been preserved for posterity, Enoch. Nothing is known about Enoch except that his father tried to build a city named after him. Enoch (second generation) was the father of Irad (third generation) who was the father of Mechuyael (fourth generation) who was the father of Mesushael (fifth generation) was was the father of Lemech (sixth generation). Nothing more is known about Irad, Mechuyael, or Mesushael.

Significantly, the names of Irad, Mechuyael, and Mesushael denote Divine punishment of one kind or another. Irad means "one who is driven out." Mechuyael means "one whom God has blotted out." And Mesushael means "one whom God has made weak." Since the names given children often are indicative of the inner feelings of the name-givers, it may be assumed that some of Cain's immediate descendants were not very proud of their family background.

Lemech had two wives, Ada and Tsila.

Lemech may be considered the founder of the social institution known as polygamy, since, according to the Biblical record, none of his predecessors had more than one wife. The institution of polygamy continued to exist among the Jewish people for a long time on a quite respectable basis. However, there was a limit. The Talmud decreed that no man was to have more than four wives simultaneously. Polygamy was not absolutely forbidden for Ashkenazic (North European) Jews until about the year 1000 of the Christian Era. Although frowned upon almost universally by the Jews of the twentieth century, occasional polygamous marriages are still to be found among Sephardic (South European, African, Oriental) Jews in North Africa and the Near East.

Ada means "she who is bedecked with jewels." Tsila means

"she who sits in the shadow." The names of these two ladies seem to have been without import because Tsila was her husband's favorite and Ada did the housework. Tsila sat by his side bedecked with jewels and Ada sat in the shadows, lonely, despised, and neglected. Like many young men during the early years of married life, Lemech was more interested in enjoying himself than he was in begetting children. In order to have the kind of pleasure he liked best as often as possible and with as little inconvenience as possible, he used to give Tsila a potion of herbs to drink periodically to prevent her from becoming pregnant. She wore the finest clothes and ate the best foods and she was never expected to do any menial housework. Her function in the establishment was to provide Lemech with sensory satisfactions and she functioned effectively and often. Ada cooked her husband's meals, made and mended his garments, washed, scrubbed, and cleaned from morning to night. For all the affection and attention that her husband gave her, she might just as well have been a widow.

This was the state of affairs in Lemech's household during the first few years of his married life. But, after a while, he grew weary of this kind of housekeeping. He decided that the time had arrived for him to become, in the fullest sense, a family man. So, having reached this decision, he announced to Ada and to Tsila that he was going to put aside his present selfish, frivolous, empty existence and he was going to devote himself henceforth to the task of being a good father and rearing worthy sons and daughters. But how can one devote oneself to one's children if one has no children? Lemech said to his wives, "We must correct this situation at once.

We must take immediate measures to provide ourselves with a satisfactory number of offspring so that we may assume our proper places in society as dedicated mothers and as dutiful father."

This declaration produced a totally unexpected reaction. Lemech's wives revolted. Ada and Tsila refused, positively and absolutely, to engage in sexual relations with their husband for the purpose of having children. Why? Because God had promised to protect Cain for only seven generations. Six generations had now come and gone. Any children whom they would bear would be Cain's seventh generation and they had a strong premonition that, in this seventh generation, some great catastrophe was destined to be visited upon Cain and upon his family. They refused firmly to bring into the world children who seemed to be doomed, from the very beginning, to face a mysterious yet certain and dreadful fate.

"What kind of silly talk is this?" bellowed Lemech. "Listen to me, you foolish women. In the first place, God has said He is going to take care of Cain for seven complete generations, and our children will only be the seventh generation. Whatever is going to happen will not happen in our children's time but, at the very earliest, in the days of our children's children, the eighth generation. In the second place, why should God bother us? He has said that He will punish anyone who tries to kill Cain. Until now I have not tried to kill him and I certainly have no desire or intention of doing so in the future. Furthermore, why should we think that just because God said that He will protect Cain for seven generations that His promise will last for only seven generations? If God wants to, He can let Cain and all of us live on for seventy seven generations or seven hundred seventy seven or forever. And did not Adam tell us that one of God's first instructions for Man was 'Be fruitful and multiply and fill the earth'? How can we expect God to show us His favor and His mercy if we do not carry out His wishes?"

Lemech cajoled, argued, pleaded, threatened, begged. It was useless. Ada and Tsila were adamant. To appease a male's sensual hunger was one thing but to produce children in a time when God was likely to withdraw His protection from them and their dear ones! That was a wickedness with which they would have nothing to do, absolutely and positively.

Finally, Lemech realized that it would be fruitless to argue with them further. So he approached the matter differently. "Let us go to Father Adam to discuss this with him," he said. "He has lived long. He is full of wisdom. He will help us to solve this problem." The women agreed. Together they went to Father Adam.

Adam listened carefully. Then he said, "Why are you young women trying to play God? How can you tell what God intends to do next year or in the next generation or in the next ten thousand years? You tend to your business and let God tend to His. Your business is to be good wives and good mothers and good housekeepers. You have a duty to your husband: to make yourselves pleasing to him and to satisfy him and to bear him healthy children. You cannot deny your husband his marital due. That would go contrary to the laws of both Nature and Man. Your husband has a Divine mandate to plant his seed in your soil. His are the privileges of sowing and of reaping. Yours are the responsibilities of fertilization and maturation. Man has the right to expect Woman to submit to him at any time that her body is physically and spiritually prepared, in order that the Divine command to 'be fruitful and multiply' may be fulfilled."

"And has Woman no privileges in this matter?" demanded Ada and Tsila. "Is this to be eternally a one-sided proposition, always weighted down in favor of Man?"

"There is no doubt," replied Adam, "that, theologically and biologically, this is Man's world and no amount of rebelling, complaining, or scheming on the part of Woman will serve to change the theological or biological nature of the universe. However, Woman does have certain rights in the matter of sexual relations. She may insist that her spouse treat her with dignity and respect. She may demand that her mate cohabit with her with a regularity that is governed by the state of his health and the type of his employment. But Woman must always exercise these rights in a sensitive and restrained manner. Man asks for love's satisfactions with his lips; Woman asks with her heart."

Adam's arguments sounded convincing to Ada and Tsila. His statements made good sense. But there was one factor in the situation which did not make good sense. They knew that Adam had not been living in accordance with his own preachments. He was not carrying out in his own life the principles which he was seeking to impress upon them.

"Why, Father Adam, if all this is so, have you abstained from granting Mother Eve her Womanly rights for the last one hundred thirty years?"

"I separated from Mother Eve because of my grief at the death of Abel. Because of a sin which I committed, death came into the world. Because of a sin which I committed, my beloved Abel is no more. I could not bear the thought of helping to bring more children into the world, children who would be born only to die, children who might end their days slaughtering each other, just as Cain killed Abel."

"So, Father Adam, you tell us not to play God. You tell us to live out our lives naturally as human beings in the manner which God has ordained for human beings. You tell us not to worry about the future and about what might happen to the children we may bear. You tell us all these things and you do not believe them yourself. Physician, heal yourself before you prescribe for others."

"I have not realized until now, my dear Ada and Tsila, that my own situation is such a questionable one. Your criticism of me is, indeed, quite justified."

"You say, Father Adam, that a woman is entitled to the periodic love-making of her husband. You say that she may expect her mate to cohabit with her with a regularity that is governed by the state of his health and the type of his employment. Have you been ill so continuously for the last hundred thirty years or have your business affairs kept you so occupied that you have been completely unable to devote any time to Mother Eve? Does this make sense? Is this fair? Do you have one standard of measurement by which you gauge your conduct toward your own wife and another by which you mete out advice to the other husbands and wives of the world? It seems to us that you are not in the most tenable of positions as a personal counsellor. So again we say: Physician, heal yourself before you prescribe for others."

Adam recognized quickly that they were completely right. In attempting to atone for his wrong-doing by denying himself the companionship of his wife, in seeking to prevent a repetition of the horror of fratricide by refusing to enlarge his family, he had not only been unfair to Eve but he had also set a bad example for the rest of mankind. If all people were to act as he had acted, the human race would vanish speedily and whatever purpose God had in mind when He created Man would not be accomplished. Adam determined that he would return to Eve at once in order to live with her, in the fullest sense, as husband and wife. As soon as Lemech, Ada, and Tsila departed, Adam gathered together his belongings and journeyed back to the place where dwelt his beloved Eve, whom he had not seen for one hundred thirty years, ever since the end of the mourning period for Abel.

Theirs was a joyous reunion. During the years of their separation, Adam and Eve had longed for each other in a spiritual rather than in a physical sense, because of a circumstance to be explained in the next chapter. During these years, both had had many lovers and yet they had never ceased to think of each other and, consciously or sub-consciously, to yearn for each other.

Eve became pregnant almost immediately after Adam's return. This time no miracle is recorded and we may assume that the baby took the customary nine months for its journey from genesis to exodus. No infant born in later times has been awaited by its parents with happier anticipation than was this one. Not only was this child to be a visible sign that two people truly in love with each other had been reunited but it was to be a living symbol of the rebirth of a couple's religious faith, faith in the wisdom of God and faith in the purposefulness of Man. When the baby was born, he was given the name of Seth, which means "God has appointed," because Adam and Eve said, "God has appointed this child to replace the one who was taken from us."

Adam never again left Eve. The renewed partnership was a long and happy one. Adam and Eve discovered that married life can be a lovely and meaningful experience only if a man and a woman do not expect too much from that life or from each other. They devoted themselves completely to the blessed task of providing a proper rearing for their handsome and gifted fifth child. But from time to time, their hearts were filled with pain: whenever they came into contact with or were reminded of their first-born son, wandering endlessly about, suffering, despised, hated, and condemned.

The sensible modern Jew is a thorough-going rationalist. He does not confuse belief and knowledge, theory and fact. He does not say "I am absolutely certain that God exists" because he knows that no one has yet produced an absolutely incontrovertible proof for the existence of God. He says "I believe that God exists" because no one has yet evolved a satisfactory explanation of life from which a belief in God is excluded. For him, God is an indispensable spiritual and philosophical Hypothesis, a mysterious Necessity, a necessary Mystery.

To state that one knows God as he knows his multiplication tables is to utter intellectual heresy. To claim that one comprehends the actions and reactions of God as well as he does those of his alarm-clock or his automobile or typewriter is to be guilty of mental and spiritual blasphemy.

The sensible modern Jew is an agnostic theist. He reacts scornfully to the evangelistic efforts of those who, hopelessly handicapped by chains of immutable dogma, weave webs of incomprehensible sophistries in vain efforts to snare unfettered minds. The agnostic theist strives to interpret God's will as best he can from nature, from tradition, from history, and from his own experience; but he never claims to know all the answers. To him the only type of religious approach that is intellectually acceptable is a faith which is based on a firm determination to face life realistically and to interpret the facts of existence humbly and respectfully but carefully and fearlessly.

Consequently, this sensible modern Jew rejects, as irrational and childish, the pie-from-the-sky type of miracle and any other sort of religious magic that does violence to the intellect and to the established order of Nature. Yet he believes that faith can move mountains, provided that one is speaking of the kind of human faith which generates maximum individual effort or concerted group action. He has removed from his thinking completely, as unworthy, unscientific, and preposterous, all such ancient and medieval notions as the belief in the existence of unseen corporeal percipient powers: be they demons, spirits, devils, or angels.

However, the Jewish sages of the Early and Middle Ages were not so thorough-going in their rationalism. They believed firmly that there were good and bad demons and good and bad angels. Their intellectual stand in this regard was about on a par with that of their non-Jewish contemporaries. This is one of the few areas in which these wise men failed to reach the level of modern Jewish religious thought.

During the one hundred thirty years that Adam was separated from Eve, Adam had frequent sexual relations with female demons. Many of them were impregnated by him and gave birth, in consequence, to infant demons. Eve, likewise, was visited regularly by male demons and produced a number of demonic children.

The sages state that in three ways these demons were like angels and in three ways they were like human beings. Like angels, they had wings, they could fly from one end of the earth to the other, and they had some knowledge of the future. Like human beings, they ate and drank, procreated, and died. They were all eccentric but not all evil. The generally accepted theory was that those who lived in one's house were good while those who lived out in the fields were evil. A house which prospered was believed to be inhabited by a good demon or a good spirit. A house which met with misfortune was believed to have been visited or haunted either by an evil demon or by the ghost of someone who had been abused by those who lived in the house.

The sages did not believe that the physical relationship between the First Inhabitants and the demons was either unnatural or harmful. Adam was a very saintly man for his time, says Rabbi Meir. When he saw that, through his sin, death had come into the world, he separated himself from his wife and afflicted himself in many other ways. He fasted frequently. He allowed vines from the garment of fig-leaves which he had made for himself to grow all over his body. But one could not expect a man or woman living alone in those early days, before the revelation at Sinai, to feel that it was wrong to satisfy one's sexual urges and needs by consorting with demons.

At the time of the Great Flood, the partly-human demons in the world perished together with the other human beings who were drowned. So all the descendants of the demonic offspring of Adam and Eve died in the Flood.

Rabbi Simon ben Yochai, the traditional author of the Zohar, says: "Woe unto mankind that does not know nor pay heed to nor understand the ways of the demons! Mankind is stupid because it does not comprehend that the world is full of creatures who cannot be seen and also is full of hidden objects that the eye has not been given power to behold. If all of these would perform all the wonders of which they are capable, no human being would be able to live in this world."

There is a colorful modern Jewish sect, the Chassidim, which takes the writings of Rabbi Simon very seriously. One of these Chassidim makes the following comment on Rabbi Simon's statement:

"It is clear from this passage that Rabbi Simon was thoroughly familiar with the scientific knowledge developed in recent times as a result of the discovery and use of the microscope. As a result of the use of the microscope, it is known that in the air of the world there are myriads of varieties of little creatures, the bacteria, which the eyes of men are unable to see and which are dangerous and which have the power to cause in men all kinds of serious illnesses. The knowledge of them is known as the science of bacteriology. They gather in the greatest numbers in unclean places. Everyone is in continual danger from them. All of this was hinted at by Rabbi Simon. And as for his reference to 'hidden objects,' he is referring to other matters which are yet beyond comprehension, such as other evil demons whose nature yet remains undiscovered."

UPON RETURNING home after their conference with Adam, Ada and Tsila offered no further resistance to Lemech's desire to become a father. Adam had succeeded in convincing the women that, by acceding to the wish of their husband, they were fulfilling a wifely obligation and, by opening the way to motherhood, they were showing their faith in God. In due time, Ada bore two sons, Javal and Juval, and Tsila became the mother of a son, Tuval-cain, and a daughter, Naama.

Javal and Juval are numbered among the world's righteous. Tuval-cain and Naama are listed with the wicked.

The sages say that, when a woman aspires to motherhood in order to perpetuate the human race in worthy fashion, superior children are formed in her womb. But if, at the moments of conception, there are no thoughts in the woman's mind beyond a desire to quench the passionate burning without and within, strange, evil, and destructive children will come from her. This is well illustrated, they continue, when one compares the children of Ada with those of Tsila.

JAVAL

"He is the progenitor of the shepherds who live in tents."

Javal was a nomad. He was the first to live in a tent and to move with his cattle from grazing-land to grazing-land and from water-hole to water-hole. When all the good grass and the fresh water in one locality were exhausted, he would take his family and his herds on a search for greener pastures and purer springs. This differed from Abel's work-pattern. Abel lived all his life in one place. Every evening, after his labors were finished, Abel would leave his herds and return home. Abel slept in a house at a distance from his cattle. Javal slept in a tent, surrounded by his cattle.

Thus Javal set a worthy example for Moses, David, and many another of the leaders, teachers, and prophets of Israel who likewise were wandering shepherds by occupation and, in the course of their years of roaming, developed the religious philosophies and the qualities of leadership which enabled them to be of great service to their people.

JUVAL

"He was the first of those who play upon stringed instruments and the pipe."

There is a great difference of opinion among the sages as to the types of musical instruments upon which Juval played. Jonathan ben Uzziel says they were like the present-day zither and flute. The Talmud adds that the flute was made of brass and not of reed or wood. Onkelas contends that, in addition to the two instruments already mentioned, Juval also played the bag-pipe. Another Midrashic authority maintains that the instruments alluded to in the Bible are the pipe-organ and cymbals. Abraham ibn Ezra states that, while it is not possible to determine just what instruments are involved, Juval, without any sort of teacher, blueprint, or precedent to guide him, must have been a person of extraordinary ability to invent and manufacture such instruments all by himself and then to perform upon them in a satisfactory manner.

All agree that instrumental music is the most direct means available to mankind for becoming filled with the spirit of God. The glory of instrumental music is like the glory of the heavens; both tell of the glory of God:

Psalm 19:4-5

"There is no speech, nor are there words;
Their actual voice is not heard;
Yet their voice goes forth through all the earth,
And their words to the end of the world."

It has been said that a singing nation is a happy nation. It may be said with equal truth that a music-loving nation can never become an irreligious nation. No name deserves to stand higher, among those who have contributed genuinely to mankind's peace of soul, than that of Juval, "first of those who play upon stringed instruments and the pipes."

TUVAL-CAIN

"He devised the method of putting sharp points on instruments of bronze and iron."

These words of the Bible change the mood of the Jewish sage swiftly and completely. Of Tuval-cain he would say: No name deserves to be reviled and cursed more than does that of Tuval-cain, creator of the weapons of war.

The learned ones among the Jews are thoroughly familiar with all the arguments used by those who speak out in favor of war: War is a glorious, exciting adventure. War brings out the finest aspects of Man's character, his ability to sacrifice his own good for that of his fellow-man and his willingness to work unceasingly as a member of a team dedicated to a common cause. The greatest scientific advancements are made either in preparation for war or during the fighting of a war. As long as there are lands to be gained, women to be won, foods to be eaten, bodies to be warmed, homes to be protected, slaves to be freed, medals to be awarded, dictators to be overthrown, generals to be glamorized, and statesmen to be canonized, men will continue to go to war.

The Jewish sages know of all this. They are hardy realists and they are not soft and blindly idealistic pacifists. They believe that, when there is no other self-respecting way out, individuals and nations must fight. It is better to fight and to die than to lose one's freedom of mind or body. They are not like the inconsistent worshipper who on Sunday solemnly intones:

"Do not resist injury. If anyone strikes you on your right cheek, turn the other to him, too; and, if anyone wants to sue you for your shirt, let him have your coat, too. If anyone forces you to go with him one mile, go with him two miles";

and then, on Monday, raises his fists without hesitation against anyone whose ideas or words run counter to his basic prejudices or interests.

Despite their realistic approach to this difficult problem, learned Jews agree emphatically with the thesis that, in the final analysis, there has never been a good war and there will never be a bad peace. They do not believe that any war is inevitable or that there is any difficulty which it is not possible for men of good-will to solve amicably. They are, essentially, men of peace who hate war with all their hearts and minds and who hold in contempt anyone who does anything which contributes, in any way, to the perpetuation of the most monstrous of all the evils which plague the life of Man. Therefore, the Jew would say: No name deserves to be reviled and cursed more than does that of Tuval-cain, creator of the weapons of war.

Lemech, in accordance with the promise he had made to himself and to his wives prior to the birth of his children, did everything within his power to rear his children properly and usefully. He determined to allow each of his sons to select his own occupation, provided that there seemed to be nothing socially disadvantageous in the occupations selected. He encouraged his children to follow the lines of personal development which seemed best suited to each.

When Javal, at the age of four, began to insist that he wanted to go out at night to sleep in the meadow with the cows, Lemech smiled to himself and said, "Seems that this boy will be very much like Abel." And he was right. When Juval, while still a youngster, began to whittle on sticks, hollow them out, make holes in them, and then play tunes on them, Lemech noted this with approval and said, "Appears that this boy is not selecting a very practical vocation but he certainly is going to add greatly to other people's enjoyment of life." And he was right.

But when Tuval-cain, having not yet attained his sixth birthday, spent all morning using his father's knife to fashion himself a sharp wooden spear and then came into the house with this spear and attempted to put out his mother's eye, Lemech was temporarily non-plussed. Letting each son work out his own destiny did not seem to be such a good idea, after all. However, the more he thought about it, the more he became convinced that there is some value to the manufacture of weapons. "Just imagine how much easier it will be for us to hunt wild beasts," he said. "Instead of having to run them to death or to pull them down and then strangle them or cut their throats, as we do now, we shall be able to hide behind a thicket at the water-holes and kill them by throwing a pointed object at them. It will be less frightening and painful to the beasts and less dangerous and strenuous for us. Tuval-cain, my little hunter, you have made a great discovery. Mankind will hail you as one of its greatest benefactors. You will reflect great credit on all of us." He was wrong.

As is often the case, Womanly intuition came closer to the reality of the situation than had Manly reason. "You mean to tell me," Tsila said to her husband, "that any good can come out of that boy's trying to blind me? First thing you know, somebody will get killed because of him and his inventions."

"There you go, Tsila, just like a Woman. Right away you start worrying. He is not going to kill anybody. He is going to create sharpened objects which will make the life of the whole human race happier and easier. And what if, in some future generation, some misguided human being uses one of Tuval-cain's inventions to kill another human being? You can't blame Tuval-cain for that. Tuval-cain will not commit the murder. It will be the man who will misuse Tuval-cain's invention who will be the guilty one."

As Tuval-cain grew older, he grew ever more proficient in

his trade. He soon wearied of sharpening sticks and took to inventing processes for polishing and sharpening instruments of bronze and iron. He produced the sword, the spear, the lance, and many other weapons of war.

Adam brought death into the world and was punished for his sin. Cain introduced murder into the pattern of human living and was punished for his sin. Tuval-cain took the crimes of Adam and Cain, changed them from retail to wholesale, refined them, beautified them, and popularized them. For this he was not punished. Perhaps it is impossible to devise a fitting punishment for such a colossal crime. For murdering one man, an individual may wind up dangling from the end of a rope. For supervising the killing of thousands of men, one may be made into a hero, applauded, honored, and decorated.

The sages say that Tsila was quite appropriately the mother of Tuval-cain. Because, as a young woman, she was overly fond of sensual delights, she coarsened her character and shortened her life. Likewise, her son, through his inventions, coarsens men's characters and shortens their lives. As we shall soon learn, the example set by Tsila also had a profound effect upon the life and actions of her daughter Naama.

The sages make a clever Hebrew pun upon the name of Tuval-cain. They say that Tuval-cain "tuv al Cain," i.e., he improved upon Cain's art, the art of murder. Cain had employed only the raw products of nature to commit murder. He had not used an instrument especially fashioned for the purpose. But Tuval-cain provided mankind with swords and spears so that people might accommodate themselves more readily to the task of killing each other. Tuval-cain made the sin of Cain more spicy, as a cook adds condiments when the pot has reached the boiling point so that the food may be more tasty. And what were the spices added by Tuval-cain? He taught mankind how to kill scientifically and he made wholesale murder respectable.

NAAMA

"She was the sister of Tuval-cain."

The name Naama is derived from an ancient Semitic word which can have any one of the following meanings: pleasant, easy, plentiful. These words describe exactly the most outstanding characteristics of Naama's favorite occupation. She was the forerunner of all who pursue what has often been referred to as the world's second oldest profession. Her manner of performance was so proficient that she won for herself a motley host of lovers and the sort of eternal reputation which only the most indefatigable of her kind would ever seek to equal.

The fact that she was a female made Naama very happy.

Naama accepted, joyfully and unhesitatingly, an historical and biological truth which many women resent deeply: The primary reasons for Woman's existence seem to be to assist in the perpetuation of the human species and to furnish carnal pleasure to Man. If God had merely wanted to furnish Adam with a companion, He could have created another Man. If He had wished to make sure that Adam would have sufficient intellectual stimulation, this, too, could have been done through an additional Man. Mere companionship or intellectual stimulation would not have accomplished the desired results. God designedly created another human being who,

(132)

together with Man, would form a *team*. The Hebrew phrase
in the Bible, in Genesis 2:18, which asserts this is often mis-
interpreted. The phrase is "ezer k'negdo," which is usually
said to mean that God wanted to give Adam "someone like
himself" or "a comrade." Its real meaning is that God determined to present Adam with "his opposite number," with a
person who would complement his own functions, needs, and
longings so completely that together they would make the perfect human team. But matters were so arranged, theologically
and biologically, that Man would serve perpetually as team-
captain.
Some women do not like this. They resent the fact that they are
women and, consciously or sub-consciously, they seek to gain
a foothold in those areas of activity which are primarily the
responsibility of Man. Such females insist that Man should
appreciate Woman's mind more than he desires her body and
that the highest type of love between Man and Woman is
that in which sex plays no part but the couple becomes as one
through joint contemplation of some abstract ideal. Nonsense!
This point of view may be the best substitute available to a
married couple on its golden wedding anniversary but, during the years when the blood is warm and the spirits are high,
there is no substitute for the ecstatic embrace of a Man and
a Woman who are attracted to each other by yielding flesh,
firm muscle, and the eager physical desire of each for the
other.

Naama not only welcomed her biological destiny; she rev-
elled in it. She did her best to please the males and to replen-
ish the species. Her love-partner's ancestry, appearance,
education, occupation, and life-philosophy were of no concern to her. As long as he was a male, she was content. She
was, indeed, a fitting daughter for Tsila and suitable sister
for Tuval-cain. She was the ideal camp-follower, the girl

that soldiers have dreamed about and sought out since the dawn of history.

Naama was very beautiful. Her make-up, costumes, and leisurely manner of walking were all designed to attract the attention and arouse the lust of every passing male. It was she who caused some of the angels to give up their heavenly duties and privileges, put aside their wings, and come down to earth to dwell with the daughters of men. She seduced two of the leaders of the angelic band, Uzza and Azael. The account of this exploit which these two relayed back to their fellow-angels was so sensational that other angels quickly came down to Earth to seek the delightful pleasure whose like was not known within the portals of the heavenly abode.

This unique accomplishment did not cause Naama to become haughty and imperious and to refuse her favors to those of more humble origin. She went right on furnishing pleasant, easy, and plenteous satisfaction to all manner of men, spirits, and demons. From these numerous relationships, she produced all manner of children, human and demonic. Because Adam and Eve were good human beings, their spirit-children were half-human and half-demonic and, as has been stated, they perished with the rest of humanity at the time of the Great Flood. But because Naama was wicked, her spirit-children were entirely demonic in character and live on to this day. The nature of the current activities of Naama's spirit-children will be described presently.

Naama could also sing. She was the first professional chanteuse. On festive occasions, she sang naughty and profane songs to the accompaniment of the beating of the timbrel.

At funerals, she was paid to lead the mourners in wailing for the passing of the deceased.

There is an erroneous tradition extant that she finally married Noah. This is impossible for a number of reasons. In the first place, she was much older than Noah. In the second place, a good man like Noah probably would not have married a woman with whom half the world had slept. In the third place, Naama married Shemadon, a demon, an individual who fitted in with her background and character much better than did Noah. One of the best known children produced from this union was Ashmodai, the evil spirit who makes matters more difficult for poorly prepared couples on their wedding night and from whom King Solomon wrested the famous Shamir worm, which he then used in the construction of the Holy Temple.

As for Naama's other spirit-children: The Midrash states that whenever a little child, in its sleep, has a coughing spell, it is because one of Naama's male demon-children is trying to kill the child. And whenever a man, sleeping by himself, has a nocturnal emission, it is because one of Naama's female demon-children has gotten into bed with him, wrapped herself about him and had sexual relations with him. And the perfect female about whom the man dreams while this is occurring, the female who is the physical composite of all the most beautiful women who have ever lived, is, of course, the female demon's ancestor, Naama.

THE YEARS rolled by. Javal, Juval, and Tuval-cain grew to manhood. Naama left home and found acceptance under every tree and in every alley. Tsila, beset by the infirmities and limitations which afflict willing women at an earlier age than they handicap the prowling male, finally had to sit on the side-lines and watch others play the game in which she had been a youthful and agile star. Ada at long last found that happiness and serenity which comes in the twilight of life to those who have never ascended to the heights and therefore never need feel the shame or bitterness of being forced back to the common level. Lemech became blind and had to be led around by the hand. But he was still very much the master of his household and he was treated by his wives and his sons with loving respect. And Cain? Poor Cain. He continued to wander through the East, dreaming dreams and scheming schemes, wearily struggling on toward the distant mirage of family power and fame and toward the surer goal that he reached each Friday night when three stars appeared in the heavens, the blessed twenty-four-hour relief of the Sabbath, which meant a temporary end to bodily pain and mental turmoil and a chance for a joyous reunion with his patient wife and his large menage of progeny's progeny.

One day Lemech asked Tuval-cain to take him out into

the forest so that he might have an opportunity to test Tuval-cain's latest invention, a device which could be used either for amusement, hunting dangerous animals, or killing men, depending upon the mood and purpose of the user. Tuval-cain had given the device the quite descriptive name of bow-and-arrow. He had learned more than just how to bend the bow and sharpen the arrow. He had managed to shape and arrange the arrow-feathers so that the arrow would fly swift and straight and he had discovered how to tip the point of the arrow with metal and poison so that it would penetrate and kill any living thing it struck. These were, indeed, re-markable achievements, as any scientist will tell you.

Wishing to please his father, Tuval-cain took the day off from his normal labors, picked up his newest contrivance, and led his father out into the woods. "As soon as we come across a creature of the forest," Lemech instructed his son, "turn me in the direction of the animal, hand me the bow-and-arrow, and guide my hand so that the arrow will go straight into its heart." After they had been walking for a while, they heard something approaching. Both stopped, tense with excitement and expectation. "What is it?" whispered Lemech. "Can't tell yet," answered Tuval-cain. There was another moment of nervous silence. Then Tuval-cain said in a low voice, "Here it comes. Can't quite make out what it is. Certainly is a peculiar looking kind of animal."

"Let's kill him," replied Lemech. Tuval-cain turned his father in the direction of the creature, placed the bow in his hand, inserted the arrow in the bowstring and directed, "Draw the arrow back as far as you can and then let it fly." Lemech steadied the arrow with his left hand and, with his right hand, drew back the arrow until he felt the bowstring grow taut. Then, wham! he shot the arrow from the bow. It flew straight toward the creature and felled it as though it had been struck with a heavy mallet. "You got him," yelled Tuval-cain. "Hurray!" yelled Lemech. "Go, see what it is, son!"

Tuval-cain ran to the fallen form. As he approached the carcass, he saw that it was the body of an old man, with a long horn coming out of the centre of his forehead. Shocked, he returned to his father. "Father," he said, "I have terrible news for you. We have just killed grandfather Cain!" "You mean," cried Lemech, "that that creature you thought was an animal was really grandfather Cain?" "Yes," answered Tuval-cain. "Oh, woe is me!" cried Lemech. As he uttered these words, he smote his large hands together suddenly and with such force that Tuval-cain, who was standing in front of him, was struck by the fists of his father, was hurled to the ground, hit his head against a rock, fractured his skull, and died immediately. . . .

When evening came, Lemech and Tuval-cain failed to return home. Ada, Tsila, Javal, and Juval went into the forest to look for them. After they had searched for a while, they heard someone groaning. Proceeding in the direction of the sound, they came upon a strange and pitiful sight. Blind Lemech was crawling around the body of Tuval-cain, beseeching his son to speak to him and to help him show the proper respect to grandfather Cain. Lemech's hands and clothes were stained by grass and dirt. His face was pale. His body was shaking. He was in a state of profound mental and physical agony.

The body of Cain was lying where it had fallen. Upon his face there was a look of infinite quiet and contentment. Death had come unexpectedly and swiftly and had soon wiped away all the marks of punishment and of pain. Life had been for Cain a bitter and a turbulent experience. Death had brought him oft-longed-for rest and a never-to-be-broken Sabbath peace.

God had protected Cain until the seventh generation and then had withdrawn His protection. Lemech was not to blame. He was, literally and figuratively, a blind instrument of God's will. He had been used in a way in which the forces of nature, the thrusts of nations, and the emotions of men are used continually: as unwitting agents to put into effect the decisions of God.

From this last statement, one might draw the conclusion that Judaism teaches that everything is foreordained and that the individual has no control over his actions and no responsibility for them. This would be an entirely erroneous conclusion.

Judaism teaches that every human being is fully responsible for every deed that he performs *deliberately* and *knowingly*. But Judaism guards one against grieving over that which cannot be foreseen or avoided.

The good person who has done his very best and has succeeded; the good person who has done his very best and has failed; the good person who, by sheer accident, has done nobly; the good person who, unintentionally, has hurt or harmed—all of them will explain what has happened in the same simple way: "God willed that it should be so. Blessed be the name of God." Does this plain, sturdy affirmation of faith mean that Judaism denies to Man all freedom and responsibility? Does it mean that Judaism teaches that everything that happens has been pre-determined by God? Not at all.

The sages say: "There is an angel which appears before God at the moment that a human being is conceived and says to Him: 'What sort of fate is in store for this person? Shall it be a male or a female, strong or weak, rich or poor, short or tall, ugly or beautiful?' God decides all these and many other matters in advance. But the angel never asks God the question: 'Shall this person be righteous or wicked?' for that is a matter which God does not decide in advance. Everything is ordained by God except whether or not an individual person is to follow the will and law of God. This is a matter which each individual is permitted to decide for himself."

And so within certain limits, rather narrow limits to be sure, each individual is given the privilege of being the master of his own fate and the captain of his own soul. Man is given the opportunity frequently to choose one of a number of ethical alternatives and he is held personally responsible for that which he selects. Through study of the Torah and Nature and human experience, he has a quite good idea of the choice which will find favor in God's sight. The word "God" in the last sentence should be underlined strongly. The righteous person will never do anything because he thinks "This is what Man says God wants me to do" but he will be guided always by the conviction that "This is what God says He wants me to do." If a person's ethical and spiritual choices do not accord with those indicated by the Torah, Nature, and human experience, he must be prepared to face the unpleasant consequences of his acts without complaint and without loss of faith in God.

It has been stated in these pages before and it cannot be stated too often: God does not exist to help to bring to fruition the plans of Man. Man exists to help to carry forward a plan designed by God. God does not exist to serve us. We exist to serve Him. To one who lives only for himself, this is an onerous situation; but to one who has dedicated his life to his fellow-men and to his God, this is the heart of religion, the meaning and purpose of human striving, the sum and substance of all that Judaism teaches and of all that man-kind needs to believe.

Lemech never recovered from the tragic experience of killing his wandering ancestor and his youngest son. To the end of his life, he would explain to anyone who would listen that he did not mean to kill Cain and Tuval-cain and that the whole thing was a dreadful accident. Lemech was fearful that God would punish both him and his family very severely for what he had done. Now it became the turn of his wives and of Javal and Juval to attempt to restore to him the faith in God's goodness, justice, and wisdom which, years before, he had helped to instil in Ada and Tsila. "Consider," they said to him, "that Cain, who committed murder deliberately, was allowed to live for seven generations. Is it not logical then to believe that you, who killed your dear ones acci-dentally, will live on for many more than seven generations? Why do you worry so? God will not hold you nor your de-scendants responsible for this tragedy." But their pleading and argument accomplished nothing. To the end of his days, Lemech grieved and lamented over the deaths he had caused. He went to his grave convinced that his family would ulti-mately be destroyed because of his sin.

The body of Tuval-cain was given a decent burial but the remains of Cain could not be buried. Because the Earth had sought to protect Cain after he killed Abel, she was not allowed to receive her former master's body. The corpse of Cain was placed in a tree. There it remained for many generations. Hundreds of years later, it was battered to pieces and destroyed by the waters of the Great Flood.

THE GENERATIONS OF CAINITES who lived in the centuries
which followed improved upon the patterns of violence and
sexual excess bequeathed to them by Tuval-cain and Naama.
The cardinal sins of later times, murder, incest, and idolatry,
were the common order of the day.

One man often killed another just to satisfy the blood-lust
which had welled up within him. People liked to watch each
other die, especially if death came slowly and painfully.
Great satisfaction was derived also from observing the suffering of living creatures. It was considered fine sport to flog
a slave or pull an old man's beard or throw a kitten into a
river. The concern of each for all grew less and less and the
love of each for self grew more and more. Rugged individualism was on the march.

As far as the sex-life of the species was concerned: All
the sex tabus were violated. Men did not hesitate to attach
themselves to anyone to whom they took a fancy, their
mothers, their daughters, the wives of their friends, their
sons, their business associates, sheep herders, camel drivers,
anybody. Nor did they care where they were or who saw
them, whether it was in private or in public, at home or on
the street or in the woods or at the beach or in their houses
of worship or any place. And the women were just as bad
as the men.

It was in this evil time that idol-worship got its start. The "scientific" reasoning of that day went something like this: God neither needs nor desires the worship of Man because God is so very powerful and so very far away. Since it has been said that God created Man in His image according to His likeness, it is logical to believe that Man looks something like God and behaves somewhat like God, and, therefore, may be regarded, if not as God, at least as god and worshipped as such. It follows, then, that God must have a multitude of faces and is capable of behaving in an uncountable number of unpredictable ways. It also follows that one way in which society may demonstrate the depth of its religiosity is by carving out statues of the more beautiful and prominent human gods, placing them in conspicuous public locations, and instructing its citizens to stop and kneel before these statues whenever filled with the mood, desire, or need for prayer or for affirmation of patriotic zeal or national solidarity.

Furthermore, since God created the stars and planets to govern the course of the Earth and since they adorn the heavens so beautifully, they, too, are worthy of being praised and honored. Therefore mankind also began to erect temples to the stars and planets and to pray to them and to offer sacrifices to them.

It is not that these early idolaters were without a belief in the power and majesty of God. It was just that they thought that God is so distant from and so disinterested in what goes on on Earth that it would be much more practical and fruitful to worship the human beings and the natural phenomena whom He had appointed as His overseers. However, after this form of worship had continued for a while, the people were no longer aware of the chain of logic which had impelled their forefathers to institute the system of idolatry. They lost all awareness of God and they began to regard the heavenly bodies and the statues as the actual creators and rulers of Earth.

There were a few righteous people, including Enosh the son of Seth, who tried occasionally to turn the people from their wicked ways, but the efforts of such were scorned and ridiculed. The situation finally reached a point where every person in the world was thoroughly steeped in wickedness, with the exception of one small family which still retained a remnant of decency and kindness and true religion. This family consisted of Noah and his wife, their three sons, Shem, Ham, and Japheth, and the sons' wives.

* * * * * *

God looked down sadly at the predicament into which the human race had gotten itself. He had entertained such high hopes for it. He even thought, at one time, of making Adam the father of the twelve sons from whom would come the Twelve Tribes of Israel. God had given Adam two sons as a test of his administrative ability; and he had been unable to prevent one son from killing the other. So the idea of giving him many more sons was abandoned. But God had still nourished the thought that mankind would eventually put aside that which is evil and choose that which is good. He had been encouraged by the lives of Seth and Javal and Juval, especially by Javal and Juval. If the Cainites could produce such fine people, everything would surely turn out all right. But it was not to be. Mankind kept getting worse and worse. There was just no point in allowing this miserable situation to continue.

God sent for Satan. "Satan, My friend," He said, "you have done your work too well. These Earth-people have succumbed so completely to the Evil Inclination that they are beyond redemption. I have no choice. I must destroy them and start this humanity-project all over again."

Satan shook his head sorrowfully. "You are right, Master. But spare Noah and his family. Of all mankind, they are the only ones who have resisted some of my blandishments successfully."

"I don't trust Noah, Satan. He seems to have a weakness for strong drink."

"Let him live, Master. What do you expect these human beings to be—angels? When You want angels, create angels; and when You want human beings, create human beings; but don't confuse the one with the other."

"All right, Satan. So be it. I'll spare Noah and his family and let them start off the next human race. But before that happens, I am going to make a few changes in the nature of things. I am going to add a few details which I overlooked when I created the Earth and its earliest inhabitants."

"What details, Master?"

"Well, it has become very clear, as this first race of people has developed, that they have become more and more interested in themselves and less and less interested in each other. That is the main reason why I am erasing this group from My thinking and am beginning all over again.

"The purpose which I had in mind when I created Man can only be achieved if Man becomes progressively more and more social-minded and less and less egocentric. The more of an individualist Man becomes, the farther he retreats from the role for which I fashioned him.

"This new race which will be fathered by Noah and his sons will have to cope with the following conditions which have been unknown on Earth until now: 1. Their produce will rot; 2. Their dead will smell; and 3. The dead will be quickly forgotten. These new factors should help to convince Man that he lives not for himself alone and that the primary reason for his existence is to serve his fellow-men and Me.

"If those who will control the world's produce try to hoard it in order to increase their wealth and power, their produce will rot.

"If anyone becomes unmindful of his littleness and his transciency and becomes bloated with a sense of self-importance, the stench of death will help to deflate him.

"In order that each human being may find his allotted place in the pattern of life and, having finished his work, may return speedily to the oblivion from whence he came, it is My desire that henceforth the dead are to be quickly forgotten. Thus none will be exalted above his fellow-men and each will get on, modestly and willingly, with the task which life has assigned to him."

"Master, You say that the dead are to be forgotten quickly. Just how soon is 'quickly'?"

"What a question! 'Quickly' means just that. A million years more, a million years less. A few years one way or the other. Why be concerned about such a trivial matter as Time?"

"And, Master, what about the living? Shall Man have nothing to look forward to save the certainty of utter extinction?"

"Ah, My friend, men will come and men will go but Man will endure until he has fulfilled the purpose for which I created him."

"And what is that purpose, Master?"

"That, good Satan, is the key-riddle of the Universe, a riddle which even you are not yet clever enough to solve nor wise enough to understand."

The principal sources used in the writing of CAIN: SON OF THE SERPENT are:

BIBLE

Book of Genesis, chapter 4

and the following Biblical commentaries:

Abraham ben Meir ibn Ezra, Spain, 1092-1167
Isaac ben Judah Abravanel, Spain, 1437-1508
Joseph Karo, Palestine, 1488-1575
K'ley Yakar, Ephraim Solomon ben Aharon, Bohemia (now Czecho-slovakia), 1550-1619
Maharshal, Solomon Lurya, Poland, 1510-1573
Or Hachayim, Chayim ben Moses Attar, Italy, 1696-1743
Ramban, Moses ben Nachman, Spain, 1195-1270
Rashi, Solomon Isaac, France, 1040-1105
Sforno, Obadiah ben Jacob of Sforno, Italy, c.1475-c.1550
Sha'ar Bas Rabim, Chayim Lev Fenster, Russia, 1902
Sifse Chachamim, Shabbatai ben Joseph Bass, Netherlands, 1641-1718
Targum Onkelas, Babylonia, 3rd Christian century, author unknown
Targum Yehonasan ben Uzziel or Targum Yerushalmi No. 1, Palestine, c.4th Christian century, author unknown
Targum Yerushalmi No. 2, not earlier than 7th Christian century, author unknown.

TALMUD

Written in Babylonia from about the fifth pre-Christian century to the sixth Christian century. The following passages are used: Avoda Zara 8b; Avos d'Rabbi Nasan 1, 16, 31; Baba Basra 16b; Berachos 61a; Eruvin 18b, 100b; Kesubos 62ab; Kiddushin 30b; Nedarim 41a; Nida 30b; Pesachim 54b; Sanhedrin 29a, 37ab, 38b, 58b, 59b, 74a, 91b; Shabbas 28b, 110a, 118b, 146a; Sota 9ab; Succa 52a; Yevamos 44a, 62a, 103b; and Yoma 19b, 52a;

and the following Talmudic commentaries:

Ahavas Eson, Abraham of Minsk, Poland, date not known
Anaf Yosef, Enoch Zundel ben Joseph, Russia, died 1867
Ets Yosef, Enoch Zundel ben Joseph, Russia, died 1867
Harif, Isaac Alfasi, Morocco, 1013-1103
Iyun Yaakov, Jacob ben Joseph Reischer, France, died 1733
Maharshaw, Samuel Edels, Poland, 1551-1631
Rashi, Solomon Isaac, France, 1040-1105
Tosaphos, many authors, France, Germany, and Italy, 12th to 14th centuries.

MIDRASH

These classical compilations of midrashic material appeared in Palestine and Europe from about the 3rd to the 13th centuries. The essential facts about each and the passages used from each are:

Midrash Rabba

Bamidbar Rabba, Europe, c.12th century, author unknown: 7:5; 20:6
Bereshis Rabba, Palestine, between 4th and 6th centuries, author unknown: 3:7; 9:2, 7; 17:4, 7; 18:4, 6; 19:1, 3, 4, 7, 11; 20:11; 22:2, 3, 5, 6, 7, 8, 9, 10, 11, 12, 13; 23:1, 2, 3, 4, 5, 6, 7; 24:5, 6; 26:5; 32:2, 5
Devarim Rabba, country of origin uncertain, c.900, author unknown: 8:1

Cain: Son of the Serpent

Koheles Rabba, country of origin uncertain, c.8th century or later, author unknown: 3:11; 4:13; 6:3
Sh'mos Rabba, country of origin uncertain, c.11th or 12th centuries, author unknown: 31:17
Vayikra Rabba, Palestine, c.7th century, author unknown: 10:5; 17:2; 27:5

and the following commentaries on Midrash Rabba:

Matnos Kehuna, Baer Ashkenazi, Poland, c.1550-c.1610
Nezer Hakodesh, Yechiel Michal ben Uzziel Glogau, Germany, died 1730
Perush Meharzu, Zev Wolf ben Israel Issar Einhorn, Russia, died 1862
Rashi, Solomon Isaac, France, 1040-1105
Yafe Toar, Samuel ben Isaac Ashkenazi Jaffe, Italy, died 1580
Y'de Moshe, Jacob Moses Ashkenazi, date not known.

Mechilta, Palestine, c.3rd century, author unknown
Shira 9:2.

Midrash Tanchuma, country of origin uncertain, c.10th or 11th centuries, author unknown
Behar 1; Bereshis 9, 10, 11; Chukas 6; Emor 9; Metsora 4; Mishpatim 13: Noach 13; Pikkudey 3.

and the commentary on Midrash Tanchuma known as Ets Yosef by Enoch Zundel ben Joseph, Russia, died 1867.

Midrash Tehillim, Palestine, c.11th or 12th centuries, author unknown: 1:9; 9:1, 2; 22:17; 34:1; 92:1.

Pirke Rabbi Eliezar, Palestine or Syria, c.8th century, author unknown: Chapters 13, 19, 21, 22, 23, 31, 35, and 42

and the commentary on Pirke Rabbi Eliezar known as Biur Maspik of unknown authorship and date.

Yalkut Shemoni, compiled by Simon the Preacher, Germany, 13th century: Section II:148.

Zohar or Midrash of Rabbi Simon ben Yochai, compiled by Moses ben Shem Tov de Leon, Spain, 1250-1305: Comments on Genesis, chapter 4

and the commentary on the Zohar known as Ziv Ha-zohar.

PAGE-BY-PAGE LISTING OF SOURCES

This is a list of the midrashic sources that were employed in the preparation of various portions of the text and commentary. What of those portions for which no sources are given? It may be assumed that they are largely the product of the writer's own thoughts and imagination. In exercising the privilege of using his own intelligence and his own imagination, the writer merely walked in the way that had been laid out for him by earlier generations of midrashists.

PAGE	PARAGRAPHS	SOURCES
Chapter I		
11	3	Maharshaw to Sanhedrin 38b
	4	Sanhedrin 38b
12	1	Ahavas Eson to Sanhedrin 38b
	2-3	Bereshis Rabba 17:4
		Tanchuma Chukas 6
	4	Bereshis Rabba 17:7 and 18:4
13	2	Anaf Yosef to Sanhedrin 29a
14	1	Perush Meharzu to Bereshis Rabba 18:6
	2	Bereshis Rabba 22:2
	3	Bereshis Rabba 18:6
15	1	Perush Meharzu to Bereshis Rabba 22:12
	2	Bereshis Rabba 19:1
		Pirke Rabbi Eliezar, chapter 13
		Ziv Ha-zohar to Zohar Genesis 4:1
	3	Sota 9ab
	4	Sanhedrin 59b
16	1	Sanhedrin 59b
Chapter II		
17	1	Bereshis Rabba 19:3

Cain: Son of the Serpent

(153)

Cain: Son of the Serpent

Cain: Son of the Serpent

(157)

Cain: Son of the Serpent

Cain: Son of the Serpent